READING
MARK
FOR THE
FIRST
TIME

Wilfrid J. Harrington, OP

Paulist Press
New York / Mahwah, NJ

Cover image by Renata Sedmakova / Shutterstock.com

Cover and book design by Sharyn Banks

Library of Congress Cataloging-in-Publication Data

Harrington, Wilfrid J.
Reading Mark for the first time / Wilfrid J. Harrington, OP.
    pages cm
ISBN 978-0-8091-4843-1 (alk. paper) — ISBN 978-1-58768-280-3
1. Bible. Mark—Criticism, interpretation, etc. I. Title.
    BS2585.52.H37 2013
    226.3`06—dc23

                                                    2013016483

ISBN: 978-0-8091-4843-1 (paperback)
ISBN: 978-1-58768-280-3 (e-book)

Published by Paulist Press
997 Macarthur Boulevard
Mahwah, New Jersey 07430

www.paulistpress.com

Printed and bound in the
United States of America

CONTENTS

INTRODUCTION

Today, before we Christians begin to read a Gospel, we already know the lines of the story. It was the same at the start. The first readers or hearers of each Gospel knew the story as well as the evangelist. Each evangelist put a "spin" on a familiar story. The reader will ask: why is he telling the story like this? One of the joys of studying the Gospels is a growing appreciation of the literary sophistication of the evangelists. One repeatedly discovers something fresh to admire.

Mark is the earliest of our Gospels. It is a taut text. Behind the text is a gifted storyteller and thoughtful theologian. Increasingly, Mark has become my favorite Gospel. I believe I admire most the evangelist's realism. It further confirms my conviction that the cross is indeed the heart of Christianity—the cross as understood by Paul and Mark and the author of Revelation. Mark's theology is a theology of the cross, and Mark's Jesus is the most human in the Gospels.

The Gospel according to Mark sets the pattern of a Gospel: it is concerned with Christology (the theological

1

understanding of Jesus Christ) and discipleship. Jesus is the Son of God. He is the Son of Man—the one come to serve, the one faithful unto death. A person who has come to terms with the cross (with the meaning of Jesus' death) can know him and confess him—like the Roman centurion (see Mark 15:39). His disciples did not understand him before Calvary. The Christian reader of the first century and of today is being challenged to come to terms with the love of God shown forth in the cross of Christ.

What I propose in this book is modest. I seek, first (in Part I), to back up my appreciation of the literary sophistication of Mark by outlining his technique. I do not claim to do him full justice. I do hope that I have done enough to demonstrate that he is, indeed, a gifted storyteller and talented writer.

In Part II, I discuss the centrality of the cross to Mark's account of Jesus. Mark would be the first to acknowledge that his skill is wholly engaged in presentation of what he passionately embraced. Like Paul before him, he had found the inspiration and foundation of his life in "Jesus Christ, and him crucified" (1 Corinthians 2:2). This was no morbid fascination with suffering; rather, Mark shared the awe of Paul. This Jesus has loved me so very much that he had chosen not only to die for me but to undergo the horrible and humiliating manner of death by crucifixion. He, like Paul, "lived by the faith of the Son of God, who loved me and gave himself for me" (Galatians 2:20).

Overwhelmed by the reality of such unconditional love, Mark looked to this Jesus. He knows from the start that he has to do with one who is Messiah and Son of God (1:1). This

Jesus, wholly one of us, lived a life of authenticity. He did so as prophet. His teaching matched his praxis. He paid the price: to be misunderstood and rejected. Jesus of Nazareth, Christ (Messiah), freely gave himself to the bitter end and utterly (John 13:1) for us and for our salvation. To know him, to confess him, one must come to terms with that truth and truly embrace the reality of a death freely undertaken for our sake. And one must accept that he has also traced the path of faithful discipleship.

PART ONE

THE

STORY

CHAPTER 1

THE STORY

GOSPEL AND EVANGELIST

The Fourth Evangelist has told us the aim of an evangelist: "Now Jesus did many other signs in the presence of his disciples, which are not written in this book. But these are written so that you may come to believe that Jesus is the Messiah, the Son of God, and that through believing you may have life in his name" (John 20:30–31). He had no intention of giving us an account of the life and times of Jesus of Nazareth. His selective account of the "signs" of Jesus was written that the Christian disciple may go on believing that the historical figure, Jesus, is the Messiah of Jewish expectation, that he is Son of God. He wrote that through their faith in Jesus, Christians might find life in him. The Gospels are proclamations of the Good News, not records destined for an archive. If they do appear to concern themselves with what Jesus of Nazareth had done and said, they are aimed at Christian communities striving to live the Christian way.

7

A gospel is, in short, a Christian document addressed to Christians. All four evangelists were concerned to set out both the *story* of Jesus and also what they took to be the *significance* of his actions and teaching. In practice, each Gospel was written for a particular community, with the needs of this community firmly in mind.

Mark, it can be argued, had pioneered the gospel form, had invented the literary form known as "gospel": a narrative that tells the story of the life, teaching, death, and resurrection of Jesus of Nazareth, the Christ, the Son of God. He had wanted to present the kerygma, the proclamation of the Good News, and had hit on the design of setting it in a framework of a schematized ministry of Jesus. Mark was keenly aware that the revelation of salvation takes place in the real world of human existence. It was, then, altogether fitting that God's saving purpose should be in terms of the human life of Jesus Christ. Inspired by this insight, his Gospel, although a taut text, is subtle and complex. It could not be otherwise since the author, a brilliant storyteller and thoughtful theologian, seeks to express, in terms of a human life, the startling fact of divine presence in our world, with the tensions that truth involves.

Above all, the evangelist Mark stands side by side with the apostle Paul as a stalwart proclaimer of a *theologia crucis*— a theology of the cross. And, congenial to modern Christology, the Jesus of Mark is the most human in the Gospels. The Gospel according to Mark sets the gospel pattern: it is concerned with Christology and discipleship. Jesus is the Son of God—the "image of the invisible God" (Colossians 1:15); he is "son of man," the human one come to serve, the one faithful unto death. A person who has come to terms with the cross (with the meaning of his death) can know him and confess him—like the centurion (Mark 15:39). His disciples did not understand him before Calvary. The Christian reader of the first century, and of today, is being challenged to come to terms with the love of God shown forth in the death of Christ.

Mark had written for the community of his concern. It was a mixed community, with Christians of Gentile and of Jewish background. Sustained interest in the Gentile mission and a care to translate Jewish terms and explain Jewish customs indicate the Gentile element, which would have been predominant. But a care to do justice to the privilege of Israel is a gesture to the feelings of those whose former religion was that of Judaism. The evangelist is intent on knitting his community together. Jesus is the bond of union. Their common faith in him should, ideally, make them and keep them one. We must see if we may discover the home of this Markan community.

THE SETTING OF MARK

The Setting

The view that Mark had written in Rome about 65 CE and for people in Rome had long been the prevalent one. But it has not gone unchallenged, because the traditional data that point to this provenance and date are of uncertain worth. We are forced back to the text of the Gospel: an anonymous writing of the first Christian century. The author is not named in the Gospel; the traditional name *Mark* was quite common. Nothing in the Gospel points necessarily to Roman origin. We can be sure that "Mark" wrote for a specific community and in face of the actual circumstances of that community. We are left to tease out a plausible setting for his Gospel and its likely date.

Today we confidently set the writing of the Gospel close to the events of the Jewish War of 66–70 CE. A careful reading of Mark 13 would suggest a date soon after the Roman destruction of Jerusalem in 70 CE. In line with mounting scholarly opinion, I would propose that Mark was written to and for a Christian community somewhere in the Roman province of Syria. This would offer a setting close to the tragic events of the war. The community may even have harbored Christian refugees from the conflict, making it that more immediate.

The Gospel and the Man

"Who then is this?" (4:41). The question was wrung from the awestruck disciples of Jesus when, at his word, a great calm had fallen upon the troubled waters and their storm-tossed boat had come to rest. For Mark, that chastened crew might have been the community, the little church, for which he wrote. He wrote for people such as them, who needed to know Jesus, who wanted to understand who he really was. He wrote for Christians who doubted and were fearful: "Teacher, do you not care if we perish?" (verse 38). He wrote for Christians who did not relish the idea of being disciples of a suffering Messiah. He wrote for Christians very like ourselves. His Gospel is a tract for our time.

We may ask, What about Mark? His Gospel shows him to be a storyteller of great natural talent, a man with an eye for telling detail, an author who could effectively structure his material. Mark emerges, too, as a theologian of stature. Some have argued for a Pauline influence on Mark. It is likely that he was indeed familiar with some of Paul's letters. Whatever of that, the Christ of Mark is a Christ whom Paul would recognize, and the Gospel of Mark is one that Paul would not have disdained to call his own. Mark's Gospel is the Gospel of Jesus Christ, the "Son of God," and closes with the resounding declaration: "Truly, this man was God's Son!" (Mark 15:39). And yet his Jesus is a man who was indignant and angry, who took children into his arms, who suffered and died. This Son of Man who came "not to be served but to serve, and to give his life as a ransom for all" (10:45), is the Christ whom Paul preached: "When I came to you, brothers and sisters, I did not come proclaiming the mystery of God in lofty words of wisdom. For I decided to know nothing among you except Jesus Christ and him crucified" (1 Corinthians 2:1–2). Paul the Apostle, the first great Christian theologian, had come to terms with the scandal of the cross. Mark the evangelist is, perhaps, the next notable Christian theologian in line.

Mark's Spirituality

In current usage, spirituality is a broad and elusive term. Christian spirituality is, perhaps, best understood as *faith*, lived in *love*, sustained by *hope*. Our faith is trust in God, whose graciousness has been revealed in and through Jesus Christ. Christian life is faith-inspired life. It is a way marked by *love*—love of God and of one another. It is a *koinonia*—fellowship. Our Christian life is pilgrimage; we need to be sure that we do not journey toward a mirage. Our hope, like our faith, is based on the faithfulness of our God, the God we meet in the Son. Because of the suffering and death of the Son, and his being raised from death, our star of hope shines for us beyond suffering, beyond death itself.

Mark's Gospel is a model of Christian spirituality. Jesus displays trust in his Father and insistently calls for faith. He shows love for all, especially the marginalized, and demands that we serve one another in love. Mark's theology of the cross is, paradoxically, the surest ground of hope. The response to Jesus' cry of "God-forsakenness" was his vindication through resurrection. As for positive response to Jesus within the Gospel, that came exclusively through "marginal" figures, notably women. This should not surprise us. After all, Jesus had declared: "it is to such as these that the kingdom of God belongs" (10:14). Our response to Mark's spirituality demands humility: "Let anyone with ears to hear listen!" (4:9).

THE STORY

Plot and Characters

A gospel addressed to a Christian community has the concerns and needs of the community in mind. These are concerns and needs perceived by the evangelist (not necessarily by the recipients, or at least, not by all of them). His readers know the basic story as well as the author—they are

Christians. He makes his point by telling the story in his way. It is a story with plot and characters. Each of the evangelists tells the same story (manifestly true of the authors of the Synoptic Gospels), but the plots and emphases of the Gospels differ considerably. The events and actions of a story, its plot, regularly involve conflict; indeed, conflict (not necessarily violent conflict) is the heart of most stories. If, for instance, in a romance, all went smoothly with the lovers, there would be no story. Not only do the Gospels have plots, but the plot is, in a sense, the evangelist's interpretation of the story. As writers of narrative literature, the evangelists achieved their purpose by means of plot and characterization.

Characterization refers to the manner in which a narrative brings characters to life in a story. In literary terms, "characters" are not the same as people. In day-to-day life we know one another imperfectly. I may guess at your thoughts; I cannot really know what you are thinking. Characters can be transparent. The narrator may fully expose a character to one's readers and can permit the reader to get inside the character. Alternatively, one can present a "true" picture of any character. The Gospels, in which Jesus is a literary character, make him known to us more profoundly than he, as a person, was known to his contemporaries.

The distinction between "character" and "person" is very important. Jesus of Nazareth was a wholly historical person. He was a first-century Palestinian Jew who carried out what, he was convinced, was a God-given mission to his people. He was rejected, condemned, and executed by an alliance of Jewish religious and Roman political authorities. The "character" Jesus of the Gospels is this Jesus now viewed through Christian eyes, seen through the prism of Easter faith. Each Gospel has several characters of varying importance for the flow of the story. Jesus is always the chief character; the evangelist speaks primarily through him. Jesus carries the central message of each Gospel. And Jesus is chief spokesman of an evangelist's concern.

The Plot

As in story generally, the events and actions of the Markan story involve conflict, and Jesus is the immediate cause of the conflict. We may illustrate by looking first at conflicts between Jesus and the authorities, and then at those between Jesus and his disciples.

Jesus versus the Authorities

The authorities involved were the religious and political leaders, and in relation to them Jesus was at a disadvantage. Mark does indeed show Jesus having facile authority over evil spirits (the exorcisms) and over nature (the stilling of the storm). But Jesus' authority did not extend to lording it over people. Still, what Jesus said and did challenged directly the authorities of Israel. For their part, these authorities viewed themselves as defenders of God's law. They contended that Jesus assumed unwarranted legal authority for himself, interpreted the law in a manner they considered illegal, and disregarded many religious customs. They responded by mounting charges against him.

Jesus, for his part, had been anointed to usher in God's rule (1:9–11). The issue for him was how to get the authorities to see God's authority in his deeds and teaching. The narrator skillfully created tension and suspense. By the end of the five conflict stories (2:1—3:6) the sides are clearly established (3:6). The impending clash with the authorities is kept in sight during the journey to Jerusalem (2:27—10:52). The climactic confrontation in Jerusalem came quickly. It is noteworthy that the first accusation against Jesus was a charge of blasphemy: "Why does this man speak in this way? It is blasphemy!" (2: 7). Thus, from the start of the story, Jesus walks a tightrope. Nevertheless, the reader recognizes that Jesus is firmly in control. At the trial he himself volunteered the evidence his accusers needed. "'Are you the Messiah, the Son of the Blessed One?' Jesus said, 'I am'" (14:61–62). Jesus, not the authorities, determined his fate.

The narrator resolves the conflict with the authorities only when they condemned Jesus and put him to death. It was an ironic resolution. The authorities had unwittingly cooperated in bringing to pass God's purpose. By means of this ironic resolution, the story depicts Jesus as the real authority in Israel. The authorities condemned as blasphemy Jesus' claim to be Son of God but, since in the story Jesus' claim is true, they are the ones guilty of blasphemy. The irony is hidden from the authorities, but it is not hidden from the reader. The reader knows that Jesus will be established in power and the authorities condemned (8:28—9:1; 13:24–27, 30–32; 14:62).

Jesus and the Disciples

At stake in the conflict with the disciples is whether Jesus can make them good disciples. The disciples struggled at every point to follow Jesus but were simply overwhelmed by both him and his demands. Jesus' efforts to lead the disciples to understand were matched by their fear and their hardness of heart. Theirs was not the determined opposition to Jesus of the authorities—they were trying to be his followers. They did consistently misunderstand Jesus' teaching and ended up by failing him utterly. Yet they had followed him to Jerusalem. Jesus just could not lead his chosen disciples (effectively, the Twelve) to understand him; he could not get them to do what he expected of them. In an effort to bring them to realize how dense and blind they were, he hurled challenging questions at them (4:13, 40; 8:17–21, 33; 9:19; 14:37, 41) and was often met with silence. He tried to prepare them for his impending death and for his absence. He knew that they would fail him in Jerusalem, yet he sought to urge them to stand by him (14:37, 41–42). The outer conflict reflects an inner conflict: they want to be loyal to Jesus, but not at the cost of giving up everything, least of all their lives. The fact remains that readers of the Gospel are most likely to empathize with those same disciples. By doing so the readers come to discern their own inadequacies. They find comfort in the realization that, although the disciples failed him, Jesus remained unflinchingly faithful to them.

Jesus did not, however, manage to make them faithful disciples. They failed him, and the question remains: will they learn from their failure and, beyond his death, at last become true followers of him? When Jesus had warned his disciples of their impending failure (14:26–31) he had added a reassuring word: "After I am raised up, I will go before you to Galilee"

(14:28). That word is then caught up in the message of the "young man" at the tomb: "Go, tell his disciples and Peter that he is going before you to Galilee; there you will see him, just as he told you" (16:7). Throughout the Gospel "to see" Jesus means to have faith in him. What Mark is saying is that if the community is to "see" Jesus, now the Risen One, it must become involved in the mission to the world that "Galilee" signified. Galilee was the place of mission, the arena in which Jesus' exorcisms and healings had broken the bonds of evil. There, too, the disciples had been called and commissioned to take up Jesus' proclamation of the coming rule of God. "Galilee" is the place of universal mission. But no disciple is ready to proclaim the Gospel until she or he has walked the way to Jerusalem (10:32–34) and encountered the reality of the cross.

The Minor Characters

The narrator shows the authorities in a consistently negative light. The disciples—in practice, the Twelve—are presented in an unflattering light. In contrast, the characterization of the minor characters is firmly positive. Here, indeed, is an eye-opener. Our attention is drawn to something so obvious that it had escaped our attention. The fact is that, against both opponents and disciples, the minor characters in the Gospel steadfastly exemplify the values of the rule of God. Mark seems to be reminding his community that the sterling Christian qualities are to be found in the "simple faithful."

The narrator developed these "little people" as foils to the authorities and disciples, and as parallels to Jesus. These minor characters do measure up to Jesus' standards, especially as they exemplify the values of faith, of being least, and of willingness to serve. In the first half of the Gospel they measure up to Jesus' opening summons: "Be converted, and believe the good news." Some examples follow:

The healed Gerasene demoniac had sought to be a disciple: he "begged him that he might be with him" (5:18). Jesus' refusal of the man's generous gesture made in thankfulness—"Go home to your friends, and tell them how much the Lord [God] has done for you, and what mercy he has shown you" (verse 19)—was not really a refusal. He would not have the man with him in his immediate circle of disciples because he had a special mission for him: he was to be the first missionary to the Gentiles. And that is why, although the man was bidden to tell what God had done for him, what he in fact did was to proclaim (see 1:14; 3:14) the deed of Jesus. The notion of the Christian message to the Gentiles is close to the surface. In 7:24–30, the focus of the story of the Gentile woman is the dialogue between Jesus and the woman. The woman will not be put off by Jesus' refusal. And Jesus responded to the challenge. This quick-witted woman appealed to his sense of humor.

In the final scenes, in Jerusalem, the minor characters exemplify especially the teaching about being "servant of all." Where, before, Jesus had served others, in his time of need others served him. The consistent conduct of the "little people" stands in sharp contrast to the conduct of the Twelve. In the first half of the story, while there is no direct comparison, the minor characters emerged as examples of faith—more than could be said of the Twelve. Here the minor characters do fulfill the functions expected of disciples. Here the "little people" are highlighted. Some examples follow:

- The narrative in 10:46–52 focuses on blind Bartimaeus, who is presented as a model of faith in Jesus, in spite of discouragement, and as one who eagerly answered the call of the master and followed him on the way of discipleship.

- In the anointing of Jesus (14:3–9) the woman had made a lovely gesture, more meaningful than she knew. She, the woman disciple, displayed an understanding that the men disciples lacked (see Matthew 26:8). Her gracious deed will win her immortality (Mark 14:9).

- The women disciples in 15:40–41. The Twelve had fled (14:50). Yet Jesus had not been wholly deserted—a little group of women disciples persevered. Mark says of them: "They used to follow him and provided for him while he was in Galilee; and there were many other women who had come up with him to Jerusalem" (verse 41). The women had "followed him"—*akolouthein* is a technical term for discipleship. And they had "served" Jesus: they are authentic disciples. They are prepared to grant Jesus proper burial rites (16:1).

Henceforth, any enlightened reading of Mark's Gospel must acknowledge the major contribution of its minor characters.

Narrative Criticism

Since Mark is, indeed, a literary work, application of the method of literary criticism has provided valuable insights. In narrative criticism, "meaning" is found in the encounter between the text and the reader. While narrative critics respect the findings of historical-critical scholarship (for that matter, historical criticism and narrative criticism are complementary), they do ask different questions of the text. Historical criticism looks to the background of the text. Narrative criticism looks to the nuances of the text itself. If the answer is different in each case, it is because the question is other. Historical criticism seeks a reconstruction of "the world behind the text." Narrative criticism focuses on "the world in the text"—more simply, the text itself—and how the text addresses "the world in front of the text"—more simply, the reader's reading of the text.

Reader Response Criticism

How do we, as readers, respond to Mark's Gospel? This question brings up what has become known as reader response criticism. The focus here is not on evangelist or text but rather on the reader's response to the text. Our response is, inevitably, influenced by our own presuppositions and prejudices. These, in fact, play a larger role in interpretation than we imagine. And, of course, our modern responses are not necessarily the same as those of the first readers/hearers of the Gospel. It must ever be recognized that the text had a specific meaning for the evangelist. This must not be sacrificed to a subjective approach to the text. In short, for a balanced interpretation, we should keep in mind that evangelist, text, and reader all have their proper place.

CHAPTER 2

MARK'S LITERARY POINTERS

PLAN OF THE GOSPEL

In order to understand how the author of a book proceeds in his or her thinking, it is always good to have an idea of the general outline of the book. We can propose the following.

PART I. THE MYSTERY OF THE CHRIST
REVELATION OF JESUS' PERSON 1:14—8:30

Three sections, each beginning with a summary of the activity of Jesus and a narrative concerning the disciples, and concluding with the adoption of an attitude in regard to Jesus:

A. Jesus Welcomed and Challenged 1:14—3:6
   (1:14–15, 16–20; 3:6)

B. He Came to His Own 3:7—6:6a (3:7–12, 13–16; 6:1–6a)

C. Conclusion and Transition: Who Is Jesus? 8:27–33

PART II. THE MYSTERY OF
THE SUFFERING CHRIST

REVELATION OF JESUS' SUFFERING 8:31—16:8

A. The Way of the Son of Man 8:31—10:52
Signposted by three announcements of the fate of
the Son of Man, followed by misunderstanding by
disciples, leading to three instructions on the way
of discipleship.

B. Jesus in Jerusalem 11:1—13:37

C. Passion and Resurrection 14:1—16:8

The Endings of the Markan Gospel

Filling out the above Plan will help us better to appreciate Mark's artistry.

First, Part I: Sections A, B, and C each contain three subsections, of which each begins with a summary of the activity of Jesus and a narrative concerning the disciples, and concludes with the adoption of an attitude in regard to Jesus.

A. Jesus Welcomed and Challenged 1:14–15—3:6
(1:14–15) "Now after John was delivered up,
Jesus came to Galilee, proclaiming the good
news of God, and saying, 'The time is fulfilled,
and the kingdom of God has come near;
repent and believe in the good news.'"
(1:16–20) Call of the First Four Disciples: Simon
and Andrew, James, and John.
(3:6) "The Pharisees went out and immediately
conspired with the Herodians how to destroy
him."

B. He Came to His Own 3:7—6:6a

(3:7–12) "Jesus departed with his disciples to
the lake, and a great multitude from Galilee
followed him; hearing all that he was doing,
they came to him in great multitudes from
Judea, Jerusalem, Idumea, beyond the Jordan,
and the region around Tyre and Sidon. He
told his disciples to have a boat ready for him
because of the crowd, so that they would not,
crush him; for he had cured many, so that all
who had diseases pressed upon him to touch
him. Whenever the unclean spirits saw him,
they fell down before him and shouted, 'You
are the Son of God!' But he sternly ordered
them not to make him known."

(3:13–16) Appointment of the Twelve.

(6:1–6a) Rejection at Nazareth—"they took offense
at him." "He was amazed at their unbelief."

C. Discipleship and Mission 6:6b—8:30

(6:6b) "Then he went about the villages
teaching."

(6:7–13) Mission of the Twelve.

(8:27–30) "'But who do you say that I am?'"
Peter answered him, 'You are the Messiah.'"

Next, Part II: Sections A, B, and C.

A. The Way of the Son of Man 8:31—10:52
Signposted by three announcements of the fate of
the Son of Man, followed by misunderstanding by
disciples, leading to three instructions on the way
of discipleship.

1. The First Prediction of the Passion and Its Sequel 8:31—9:1

(8:31–32a) "Then he began to teach them that the Son of Man must undergo great suffering, and be rejected by the elders, and chief priests, and the scribes and be killed, and after three days rise again. He said all this quite openly."

(8:32b–33) "And Peter took him aside and began to rebuke him. But turning and looking at his disciples, he rebuked Peter and said, 'Get behind me, Satan! For you are setting your mind not on divine things but on human things.'"

(8:34—9:1) True Discipleship

2. The Second Prediction of the Passion and Its Sequel. 9:30—10: 31

(9:30–31) "They went out and passed through Galilee. He did not want anyone to know it; for he was teaching his disciples, saying to them, 'The Son of man is to be betrayed into human hands and they will kill him, and three days after being killed, he will rise again.'"

(9:32–34) "But they did not understand what he was saying and were afraid to ask him. Then they came to Capernaum; and when he was in the house, he asked them, 'What were you arguing about on the way?' But they were silent, for on the way they had argued with one another about who was the greatest."

(9:35–50) Jesus Instructs his Disciples.

3. The Third Prediction of the Passion and Its
   Sequel. 10:32–45

(10:32–33) "They were on the road, going up to
   Jerusalem, and Jesus was walking ahead of
   them; they were amazed, and those who
   followed him were afraid. He took the twelve
   aside again and began to tell them what was to
   happen to him, saying, 'See, we are going up
   to Jerusalem, and the Son of Man will be
   handed over to the chief priests and the
   scribes, and they will condemn him to death;
   then they will hand him over to the Gentiles;
   they will mock him, and spit upon him, and
   flog him, and kill him; and after three days he
   will rise again.'"

(10:35–41) James and John make their request:
   "Grant us to sit, one at your right hand and
   one at your left, in your glory." "When the ten
   heard this, they began to be angry with James
   and John."

(10:42–45) "So Jesus called them and said to them,
   'You know that among the gentiles those whom
   they recognize as their rulers lord it over them,
   and their great ones are tyrants over them. But
   it is not so among you; but whoever wishes to
   become great among you must be your servant,
   and whoever wishes to be first among you
   must be slave of all. For the Son of Man came

not to be served but to serve, and to give his
life a ransom for many [all].'"

In B and C the pattern is more fluid but careful compositional concern is still in evidence.

B. Jesus in Jerusalem 11:1—13:37

A notable feature is stress on endings: End of the
Temple and Its Cult (11:1–25); End of Religious
Leadership in Israel (11:27—12:44); End of
Jerusalem (13:5–23); End of the World
(13:24–27).

The End of the Temple and Its Cult (11:1–25). The
sandwich, fig tree and temple cleansing (11:12–25),
after Jesus' critical scrutiny (11:11), symbolizes the
end of the Jerusalem temple.

*The End of Religious Leadership in Israel (11:27—
12:44).* The passage 11:27–33 introduces a series of
controversy-stories akin to those of 2:1—3:6. In
sequence, Jesus reduces to silence the leaders of
Israel: chief priests, scribes, and elders, Pharisees
and Herodians, and Sadducees. Just as in chapter
11, the end of the temple had been marked, so now
is shown the end of religious leadership in Israel.

The Authority of Jesus 11:27–33

The Beloved Son 12:1–12

Question of Pharisees and Herodians 12:3–17

The Sadducees' Question 12:18–27

A Scribe's Question 12:28–34

Jesus' Question 12:35–37a

The False Religion of the Scribes 12:37b–44

Farewell Discourse Chapter 13
The End of Jerusalem 13:5–23
The End of the World 13:24–27
The Signs of the End 13:28–31

C. Passion and Death 14:1—15:47

After the Farewell Discourse (chapter 13), the curtain goes up on the final act of the drama. We have been well prepared for the denouement, not only in explicit predictions of the passion but in hints, more or less veiled, right from the beginning. The Son of Man must suffer many things. In this divine necessity Mark finds his answer to the question "Who, then, is this?" The precise answer is spoken by the Roman centurion: "Truly, this man was God's Son!" But the whole Gospel has prepared for that solemn declaration.

Marked for Death 14:1–11
The Farewell Supper 14:12–24
Prediction of Failure 14:26–31
Gethsemane 14:32–42
The Arrest 14:43–52
Before the Jewish Authorities 14:53–72
Before Pilate 15:1–15
Crucifixion 15:16–32
Death and Revelation 15:33–41
Burial 15:42–47

EPILOGUE 16:1–8

Clearly, these intricate arrangements did not just happen. We are dealing with a sophisticated and artistic author. We move to examine other literary pointers of Mark.

ARRANGEMENTS

Summary Statements

Summary statements are a feature of Mark's style. They help to move along the flow of the narrative. The first (1:14–15) opens the mission of Jesus and covers its initial stage. At the close of the specimen day at Capernaum (1:21–34), "all" the sick and possessed of the town were brought to Jesus (1:32–34). Here, for the first time, appears Mark's so-called "messianic secret"—"he would not permit the demons to speak, because they knew him." Mark firmly believed that no human being could acknowledge in faith and truth that Jesus is Son of God before the paradoxical revelation of his identity through his death on the cross. The element of secrecy concerns not Jesus' messiahship but his identity as Son of God. The divine voice, at baptism and transfiguration (1:11; 9:7), did proclaim Jesus' Sonship. "Demons" were believed to have preternatural knowledge: the unclean spirits become guides to the reader! Their being bound to silence is a reminder that to know the truth about Jesus, one must, like the Roman centurion, come to terms with the cross (15:39).

Together with the call of the Twelve (3:13–19a), the summary of 3:7–12 shows like a ray of light breaking between dark clouds of hostility (2:1—3:6 and 3:19b–35). Coming after the conflict stories, which underlined the prejudice of the scribes and Pharisees and their rejection of Jesus, the passage points again to the enthusiasm of the people and to the perception of the evil spirits who discerned what the religious authorities failed to see. A great multitude came to Jesus not only from friendly Galilee but from much farther afield. Mark is at pains to stress not only that the Jewish people crowded to Jesus from every quarter of the land, but that Jesus was evoking a response of faith among Gentiles. The theological rather than geographical interest of the evangelist is indicated in the bracket phrase "a great multitude" (verses 7–8).

After the rejection at Nazareth (6:1–6a), the terse summary—"Then he went about the villages teaching" (6:6b)—signals the continuation of his mission. The passage 6:53–56 is a generalized description of Jesus' healing activity. However, the first item, the landing at Gennesaret (verse 53), does establish a connection with the foregoing narrative of multiplication of loaves (6:35–44) and crossing the lake (6:45–46), for the sequence feeding-crossing-landing is well attested (Mark 6:30–56; 8:1–10; John 6:1–25) and is obviously traditional. The summary, as might be expected, has borrowings from and echoes of other Markan passages.

Jesus had instructed the disciples (9:35–50). The summary statement of 10:1—"He left that place and went to the region of Judea and beyond the Jordan. And crowds again gathered around him; and, as was his custom, he again taught them"—shows him again responding to the eager crowds.

Sandwich Technique

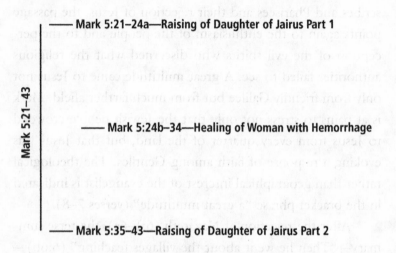

—— Mark 5:21–24a—Raising of Daughter of Jairus Part 1

Mark 5:21–43

—— Mark 5:24b–34—Healing of Woman with Hemorrhage

—— Mark 5:35–43—Raising of Daughter of Jairus Part 2

Mark has a practice of intercalating a story or episode into another story or episode, which produces a sandwich-like effect. The parts may be synonymous, or they may be antithetical—standing in contrast.

In 3:19–35, Mark's familiar "sandwich" technique points us, unerringly, toward an understanding of the passage: the episode of the scribes is sandwiched between the two sections on the family of Jesus (3:19b–21, [22–30], 31–35). It is his pointer that the two "slices" of the family story and the "filling" made up of the scribes episode be taken as a unit. In verse 21, the Nazareth family, concerned for Jesus, had come to "restrain" him. They wanted to put him away for his own good: "He has gone out of his mind." Then emerged the scribes, who came down from Jerusalem: the official Jewish reaction was to put Jesus under investigation. Verse 22 contains two accusations: Jesus was possessed by Beelzebul, an evil spirit; and his exorcisms were wrought "by the ruler of the demons," that is, Satan. These scribes had witnessed Jesus' healings; they had passed judgment. Like Job's comforters, they were complacently sure of the truth of their theology. Jesus was one who did not observe the Sabbath, one who freely associated with sinners. His conduct was an affront to the holy God. Jesus' power—they could not deny his healings—was surely not from God. That left one other source! He was casting out the malign influences that caused sickness through the power of Satan—evil itself!

The family was still about (3:31–32). Seated in the crowded house, Jesus was told that his mother and brothers were outside, wanting to speak with him—wanting to restrain him! (verse 21). Too much had happened too quickly; Jesus was lost to them, and they sensed it. Jesus looked at those inside who crowded around, hanging on his words. He had lost his natural family, but he had gained another family. His mother and brothers and sisters were not outside—they were right there before him. Those who hear and do the will of the Abba are, now and always, Jesus' brother and sister and mother—the faithful women and men of God (verses 33–35).

Nowhere else in Mark does an insertion so clearly separate two parts of a narrative as it does in 5:21–43 (21–24a, [24b–34], 35–43). Each "sandwich" of Mark is a carefully constructed unit and should be read as such. The closing words of the first part of the daughter of Jairus story (verse 24) prepare the way for the story of the woman, and the words "while he was still speaking" (verse 35) form a neat link with the second part of the main story. It is noteworthy that in these stories two women hold center stage.

Salvation and faith are the major themes of our twin narratives. Jairus was confident that at Jesus' touch his daughter would be "made well" (verse 23), and the woman was convinced that if she were to touch Jesus' garments she would be "made well" (verse 28). Each time the verb is *sozo*, which means also "to save." Jairus had pleaded that his daughter may be made well "and live." The verb *zao*, "to live," had taken on, in Christian usage, overtones of living to eternal life. The plea might be read: "That she may be saved and have eternal life." More pointedly, in verse 34, Jesus not only drew an intimate association between healing and salvation but also attributed both results to her faith: "your faith has made you well," that is, "has saved you." Mark, then, was thinking of bodily as well as spiritual healing: salvation stands in close relationship to faith. Jesus then exhorted the father of the dead girl, "Do not fear, only believe" (verse 36).

Between the sending of the Twelve on a brief mission (6:7–13) and their return (verses 30–32), Mark has, in customary fashion, inserted another episode: the death of John the Baptist (verses 14–29). The disciples, like the Baptist, prepare for Jesus' proclamation. The mission of the Baptist, like that of Jesus, will end in death: the shadow of the cross falls across the Gospel. The death of the precursor is a presage of Jesus' fate.

In 11:12–25, the account of the cleansing of the temple is inserted between two phases of the other narrative of the fig tree (11:12–14, [15–19], 20–25). Mark thereby signals that the stories should be read in relation to each other. The cursing (verse 21) becomes a judgment on the temple. On the way from Bethany to Jerusalem a leafy tree seemed to promise fruit. A typically Markan explanatory phrase explains that "it was not the season (literally, "time," *kairos*) for figs." This jarring note alerts us. We must look to a symbolic meaning: the temple tree, despite its leafy show, is barren at the time of visitation. The messiah "went to see" and found it fruitless. The prophetic gesture of Jesus, his "cleansing" of the temple (verses 15–19), symbolically disrupted the temple's cultic life. Coming after this episode, Peter's drawing of attention to the withered fig tree (verses 20–21) serves to highlight the temple crisis.

In 14:12–25, between preparation for the Supper (verses 12–16) and the Supper itself (verses 22–25), the evangelist intercalated the announcement-of-betrayal passage (verses 17–21). It is a chastening admonishment to the reader. Mark has placed the betrayal episode in the setting of eucharistic table fellowship. The Christian must ask, "Is it I?"—am I a betrayer of the Lord Jesus? (see verse 19). One is reminded of Paul in 1 Corinthians 11:28: "Examine yourselves, and only then eat of the bread and drink of the cup."

In 14:53–72, we find a poignant contrast—14:53–54, [55–65], 66–72. Peter is introduced. He had followed Jesus "at a distance"; it will shortly emerge how very far behind he is on the way of discipleship. Jesus' testimony (verses 55–65) is framed by Peter's denials (verses 53–54, 66–72). He was faithful unto death, while Peter proved unfaithful. At Caesarea

Philippi Peter had shown that he could not accept the notion of suffering messiahship (8:31–33). Now he would disassociate himself from the suffering Messiah.

Galilee

The name *Galilee* is obviously geographical. In Mark, however, it has a theological dimension. It is a symbol as much as a place. Mark had been at pains to show the wider "Galilee" as the place where crowds gathered from all of ancient Israel (3:7–8) and as the locale of the breakdown of the barrier between Jew and Gentile (7:31). There the disciples had been first assembled (1:16–20), only to fail him at the end (14:50). In his prediction of disciple failure (14:27–31), Jesus gave assurance that his community, though scattered following the fate of their shepherd, will be reconstituted by him: "After I am raised up, I will go before you to Galilee" (verse 28). He looks beyond his death and promises that the scattered flock will be gathered together again.

In 16:7, the women at the tomb were given a message, an echo of the promise of 14:28. It was a message for the disciples and especially for Peter (that is the force of the Greek). Jesus, now as risen Lord, will await them in Galilee. There they will "see" him, encounter the risen Christ. The cross was not the end. There would be a new beginning. Mark does not relate the encounter that ushered in the new phase of the Good News. The Christian community is the assurance that the promise had been fulfilled. That promise of Jesus in 14:28 is not too far removed from the commission of the Lord in Matthew 18:19: "Go therefore and make disciples of all nations."

EMPHASIS

Authors regularly have a concern for emphasis: key words and ideas need to be stressed. Modern writers have a variety of means at their disposal: for instance, italics, underlining, and bold type. Ancient writers had evolved their own techniques. Mark proves to be notably adept. Here we note his methods, which pervade his work.

Bracketing

In 2:1–12, Mark has carefully directed us to the key point of the passage. He has done so by his technique of bracketing an item of special interest by identical or near-identical frame-verses. The phrases "questioning in their hearts" (verse 6) and "raising such questions in your hearts" (verse 8) focus attention on forgiveness of sins, while the phrase "take your mat" (verses 9 and 11) emphasizes the Son of man's authority to forgive sin on earth.

In 3:7–8, we read that a great multitude came to Jesus not only from friendly Galilee but from much farther afield. While Judea, Idumea, and Perea point to broadly Jewish territory, the country about Tyre and Sidon is the wider "Galilee of the Gentiles." Mark is at pains to stress not only that the Jewish people crowded to Jesus from every quarter of the land but that Jesus was evoking a response from among Gentiles. The theological rather than the geographical interest of the evangelist is indicated by the bracket-phrase "a great multitude" (verses 7 and 8).

In the appointment of the Twelve (3:13–19a), the bracket "he appointed twelve" (verses 14 and 15) underlines the immediate role of this inner group. In the first place they are "to be with him"; they are to have a close personal relationship with Jesus, forming a new family. And from now on, the Twelve do remain constantly with him (until they fail him spectacularly in 14:50). In the second place, the Twelve were commissioned to be sent out to preach and to have authority over demons. While the evangelist had the sending out of 6:7–13 in mind, his vocabulary shows that he looked beyond it. The Greek words *apostellein,* "to send out," and *keryssein,* "to preach," are terms used by the apostolic church to designate its mission. Mark was conscious of the post-resurrection missionary situation. The Twelve were to preach and to do. The word of God is proclaimed in word and action together.

Bracketed by the repeated "Do you not understand" (verses 17 and 21), the specific recall of the two feedings of five thousand and four thousand (6:35–44; 8:1–9) is marked as the key factor of the passage 8:17–21. The unexpected emphasis—on the baskets of fragments—is a further indication that here is where we should look. We are meant to see that the number (twelve) and the *cophinos,* a basket commonly used by Jews, point to the Jewish world, while the number seven (universal) and the ordinary basket *(spyris)* indicate the Gentile world. Those of Gentile origin as well as those of Jewish origin are both at home in the household of the faith, and their fellowship is achieved in the breaking of the bread. The Christian who cannot or will not see this deserves the charge: is your heart hardened? Mark has some Jewish-Christians primarily in view. The kind of situation that Paul had encountered in Jerusalem and Antioch (Galatians 2) would also have cropped up again at a later date in other areas. It would not have been easy for Pharisaic Jews, coming to Christianity, to shrug off their ingrained prejudice and enter into warm fellowship with Gentiles. Jesus, the "one loaf," was the Messiah uniting Jew and Gentile about himself into one messianic people (see Ephesians 2:11–22).

Jesus' teaching on the hazard of riches (10:23–27) and on the reward of renunciation (verses 28–31) was provoked by the story of refusal by one whom Jesus loved to answer his call (verses 17–22). This rich man's sad departure confirmed dramatically that wealth could come between a person and the following of Jesus; the words of Jesus (verses 23–27) drive the message home. He began by stressing how difficult it is for the wealthy to enter the kingdom (verse 23) and passed quickly to the difficulty of entering the kingdom at all (verse 24). The repeated "How hard it is to enter the kingdom of God" (verses 23 and 24) frames the amazement of the disciples, who would have shared the current view that wealth was a sign of divine approval.

In the farewell discourse, chapter 13, the phrase "you do not know when the time will come" is Mark's introduction to the parable of the doorkeeper (verses 34–36). The parable is highlighted by the bracket-phrase "You do not know when the master of the house will come." Significantly, it is "the master of the house" who will come, not the "man" of verse 34; it is Christ himself. The parable is now understood in christological terms: Christ is the departing Lord and the *parousia* will mark his return.

In 14:55, we read that the Jewish authorities were looking for testimony against Jesus. The witnesses were there (verses 56–58)—false witnesses. Mark stresses their lack of agreement. The repetition "and their testimony did not agree" and "But even on this point their testimony did not agree" (verses 56b and 59) frames the temple saying: "We heard him say, 'I will destroy this temple that is made with hands, and in three days I will build another, not made with hands'" (verse 56). In this way Jesus signals the special importance of the saying. He had never threatened to destroy the temple. But he had been critical of it (11:12–25). The theme of the destruction of the temple will return in the passion narrative (15:29). And the rending of the temple curtain at the death of Jesus (verse 38) signals the effective end of the temple. God's Son is henceforth the "place" of salvation.

On the cross Jesus cried out *with a loud voice,* "My God, my God, why have you forsaken me?" (15:24). In verse 37, "Jesus gave *a loud cry* and breathed his last." Jesus had begun his mission in an encounter with Satan (1:12–13) and carried on the war in his exorcisms. The expression *phone megale* ("loud voice") occurs four times only in Mark. In 1:26 and 5:7, it is the loud cry of a demoniac, one oppressed by an evil spirit. Jesus himself now (verses 34 and 37) reacted with a loud cry to the intolerable pressure of evil, which he was bearing for us.

Peter, James, and John

The presence of Peter, James, and John—the inner core of the Twelve—with Jesus is significant. At the raising of the daughter of Jairus (5:35–43) Jesus "allowed no one to follow him except Peter, James, and John" (verse 37). Their exclusive presence is confirmation of the theological importance of the raising accomplished by Jesus. They were also alone with Jesus at the transfiguration (9:2), in Gethsemane (14:3), and, accompanied by Andrew, at the Mount of Olives as hearers of the farewell discourse (13:3). On each occasion, their presence is a pointer to the reader: here is something especially meaningful.

Kat' idian

Jesus had spoken the parable of the sower to a large crowd gathered at the lakeside (4:9). When, later, he was alone, "those who were around him along with the twelve" asked him about the parables (verse 10). "Alone" (*kata monas*) is a synonym of the characteristic Markan phrase *kat' idian,* "privately," "by themselves" (see 4:34; 6:31–32; 7:33; 9:2, 28; 13:3). Each time it occurs, the expression is used in connection with a revelation or private teaching reserved for the disciples. "Those who were about him with the twelve" (verse 10)—in the immediate context this group stands in contrast to the "those outside" of verse 11. Mark is reflecting the life and experience of his Christian community. Christians are those who understand (or who ought to understand); they are not "those outside." At the close of the parable discourse it is stated that, while Jesus spoke to the crowd in parables, "he explained everything in private to his disciples" (verse 34). In parabolic speech, Jesus revealed the kingdom (4:1–32), but his listeners must have ears to hear (verses 9, 13, and 23). Those who do hear leave themselves open to the word of God revealed in the word and person of Jesus. If he had fully instructed the insider group of disciples it is clear throughout the Gospel that they failed to understand. They did not really have ears to hear.

The Twelve had been sent on mission (6:7–13). On their return, they needed to rest (verses 30–31). "Come to a deserted place and rest awhile," Jesus invited them, and they crossed in a boat to a quiet place (verse 32). The impression is of a privileged time of retreat with Jesus. His attempt to find solitude for himself and his disciples was frustrated by the enthusiasm of the crowd, but he was not annoyed. He was deeply moved by their earnestness and their need (verse 34).

Mark sets the healing of a deaf mute (7:31–37) in the Gentile region of Decapolis. Jesus "took him aside in private." Occurrence of the expression *kat' idian* would suggest a symbolic dimension. In a Gentile setting, a man recovers his faculty of hearing and speaking (verse 35). The healing has the symbolic intent of showing that the Gentiles, once deaf and dumb toward God, are now capable of hearing God and of rendering him homage. They, too, have become heirs of the eschatological promise to Israel: "The ears of the deaf will be unstopped...and the tongue of the speechless sing for joy" (Isaiah 35:5–6).

In 9:2, the phrase "apart, by themselves" emphasizes the revelatory character of the transfiguration event (9:2–8). The presence of the three disciples Peter, James, and John underlines unmistakably the importance of the episode for Mark. At the close of the following story of the epileptic boy (9:14–27) Jesus was alone with his disciples "in a house" and they questioned him "privately." This esoteric message to the disciples is, in reality, addressed to the Christian community. "This kind can come out only through prayer" (verse 29). Jesus explains why the disciples had been unable to cope with the unclean spirit: prayer was vitally necessary as an expression of total reliance on the Lord.

The carefully designated setting (13:3–4) admirably lends to the farewell discourse (chapter 13) the solemnity and extraordinary importance Mark wants it to have. The discourse is not only "in private"; it is reserved for four of the Twelve, the four whose call is described in 1:16–20 and who have been longest with Jesus. Mark has thus alerted the reader that this reply to the disciples' question (verse 4) is of exceptional moment. And so indeed it was for Mark's community.

Jesus' Isolation through the Passion

The disciples had, consistently, failed to understand Jesus. Now, at his arrest (14:43–52), "All of them deserted him and fled" (verse 50). They forsook him and have forfeited the title of "disciple." Jesus was left all alone. His isolation is highlighted as the passion story unfolds. Peter's denial (14:66–72), with his vehement assertion that he did not know Jesus (verse 71), compounds his earlier desertion. After the sentence of crucifixion, the soldiers mocked Jesus (15:16–19). Those passing by, seeing him on the cross, derided him (verses 29–30). The chief priest and scribes mocked him (verses 31–32a). Those crucified with him also taunted him (verse 32b).

The climax occurs at verse 34: "At three o'clock Jesus cried out with a loud voice, 'Eloi, Eloi, lema sabachtani?', which means, 'My God, my God, why have you forsaken me?'" Jesus suffered the absence of God: his cry of dereliction was one of total desolation. His words "My God, my God, why have you forsaken me?" are the opening of Psalm 22, a psalm of lament. Lament is the cry of a suffering righteous person addressed to the One who can bring an end to suffering. Mark has Jesus die in total isolation, without any relieving feature at all. It would have seemed that, up to this point, Jesus' isolation could go no further: deserted by his disciples, taunted by his enemies, derided by those who hung with him, suffocating in the darkness of evil. But the worst was now: abandoned by God. His suffering was radically lonely. But his God was "my God" (verse 34). Even in this, as at Gethsemane, it was "not what I want, but what you want." Here, even more than there, the sheer humanity of Jesus was manifest. And his experience was a thoroughly human one. It underlines the difference between feeling and reality. The feeling is one of God-forsakenness. The reality, however, is that never were Father and Son more at one. It is akin to the experience of Job, who also suffered the absence of God, or of later mystics, suffering the "dark night of the soul." God had never withdrawn; the feeling is that he had.

Mark has insisted on the loneliness of Jesus during his passion: up to the moment of death he is alone, more and more alone. His intention is not only to awaken us to the poignancy of this painful solitude; he wants us to perceive in that darkness the truth that God alone saves.

CONCERNS

Misunderstanding by Disciples

It is clear from the Gospels that the disciples did not really know Jesus during the ministry. They were quite shattered by his death. In light of their encounter with him as raised from the dead they came to a fresh understanding of him. But they had, in fact, grasped more than they had realized. Matthew carries a beatitude of Jesus: "Blessed are your eyes, for they see, and your ears, for they hear" (13:16). Throughout Matthew, Luke, and John the disciples do, indeed, learn. In Mark, the situation is stolidly different. He does, it is true, have a word of Jesus quite like that in Matthew: "To you has been given the secret of the kingdom, but for those outside, everything comes in parables" (4:11). Supreme irony, because, in fact, the disciples in Mark are very much "those outside." Mark's concentration not only on the lack of understanding but also on the blatant misunderstanding by the disciples is unrelenting. Here we must remind ourselves of story and characters. In Mark the disciples of Jesus are characters who play a vital role in his theology of the cross.

A list of references is tedious. It is proposed here because this relentless pervasiveness of the misunderstanding by Jesus' disciples is a unique characteristic of Mark's Gospel. The list: 1:36–37; 4:35–41; 5:30–31; 6:35–37; 6:49–52; 8:4; 8:14–21; 8:32–33; 9:5–6; 9:9–10; 9:18–19; 9:32–34; 9:38; 10:13–14; 10:23–27; 14:10–11; 14:18–21; 14:26–31; 14:32–42; 11:50; 11:51–52; 11:66–72.

We may sum up by looking to the close of Part I of the Gospel and toward the climax of Part II.

We have observed that Mark, throughout his Gospel, had stressed the failure of disciples to understand Jesus. In all cases, they displayed lack of spiritual insight in failing to discern some hidden meaning in a word or deed of Jesus. The passage 8:14–21 is the climax of this theme in the first half of the Gospel. A series of seven questions conveys Jesus' bitter disappointment at their tardiness. "Do you not yet understand?" is the burden of the censure. Because Mark wrote with the special needs of his community in mind, he has exaggerated the obtuseness of the disciples. The drama of the episode is present from the first: "Now the disciples had forgotten to bring any bread; and they had only one loaf with them in the boat" (verse 14). The disciples, who had been actively involved in two miraculous feedings at which Jesus had satisfied the needs of large crowds, were now concerned because they were short of bread! They "had only one loaf with them in the boat"—this is just not a vivid Markan touch. The development of the passage will suggest that what the disciples failed to understand is that Jesus is the one loaf for Jews and Gentiles, as the feedings ought to have shown them.

Jesus had foretold the failure of his disciples (14:26–31). In the quotation from the prophet Zechariah one finds the key to the passage. After declaring, "strike the shepherd, that the sheep may be scattered" (Zechariah 13:7), the oracle goes on to declare that two-thirds of the shepherd-king's people will perish (13:8). The remnant will be refined and tested to become truly God's people (13:9). Jesus gives assurance that his community, too, though scattered following the fate of their shepherd, will be reconstituted by him. He looks beyond his death and promises that the scattered flock will be gathered together again. "After I am raised up, I will go before you to Galilee" (Mark 14:28). The phrase "I will go before you" could be taken as "I will lead you" or "I will go there before-hand." Either way, the disciples will meet Jesus again in Galilee (see 16:7). It would be a rebirth for them, a new beginning. "Galilee" will be, again, the area of mission—of universal mission (see 13:10).

We had not long to wait for that failure. All of the disciples had heard his predictions of suffering and death: Peter, James, and John had heard the heavenly voice (9:7); James and John had confidently declared their readiness to share his cup (10:38–39); all had asserted that they would never deny Jesus (14:31). Now, at Gethsemane (14:32–42), he took the three, Peter, James, and John to be with him in his hour of need. He asked his "disciples" to pray—they will not act as disciples. Jesus himself went apart to pray. He realized he was on his own.

It is significant that, in the Gethsemane episode, Mark has so closely woven the theme of misunderstanding by disciples with that of Jesus' testing. It is his most dramatic answer to any objection to a suffering Messiah. Jesus himself had been brought to the brink of rejecting it— "Abba, remove this cup from me!" The evangelist leaves no doubt that suffering messiahship is not easily accommodated. He knows, as fully as Paul, that the cross is foolishness and scandal (see 1 Corinthians 1:18–25). The reader is duly warned. One must watch and pray. Good intentions are not enough. Discipleship is a way of life. And the course of that way has been plotted by Jesus: "Get up, let us be going" (Mark 14:42).

The narrative of Peter's denials (14:66–72) brings the theme of misunderstanding by disciples to a head. Peter had publicly disassociated himself from Jesus. The sheep had been well and truly scattered and the stricken shepherd was wholly on his own (see 14:27). As Mark's readers see themselves in disciples who could betray and deny and forsake, they are not likely to feel complacent.

The theme of misunderstanding by disciples was of such obvious importance to Mark for two reasons. In the first place, it was central to his theology of the cross. He was convinced that only by coming to terms with the cross—the death—of Jesus might one understand him and his saving work. His disciples had not yet experienced that event. The Roman centurion was the first to perceive the truth (15:39). But Mark also had in mind frail and failing Christians. Jesus' immediate disciples did not measure up to what he would have wished. Frankly, they failed him—as Jesus had foreseen. He did not fail them. There was a new "Galilee" beyond the disaster of Jerusalem. The good news would be proclaimed, despite human failure. So it would ever be.

Jew and Gentile

Throughout his Gospel, Mark shows concern for harmony between Jewish and Gentile Christians. This interest surfaces, for instance, in the episodes of the Gerasene demoniac (5:1–20) and the Syrophoenician woman (7:24–30). The arrangement of chapters 6–8 and the intricate feature of boat journeys on the lake of Tiberias are unique to Mark.

THE ARRANGEMENT OF 6:32—8:26

We have insisted that any endeavor to understand Mark aright must take seriously his arrangement of his material. We should observe, then, that the episodes of 6:32—8:26 are ordered in two parallel series of events:

Feeding of the 5,000 (6:35–44)	Feeding of the 4,000 (8:1–9)
Crossing of the Lake (6:45–56)	Crossing of the Lake (8:10)
Controversy with Pharisees (7:1–23)	Controversy with Pharisees (8:11–13)
The Children's Bread (7:24–30)	The One Loaf (8:14–21)
Healing of a Deaf Mute (7:31–37)	Healing of a Blind Man (8:22–26)

The first multiplication of loaves takes place in Galilee and its beneficiaries are Jews. Moreover, the number "twelve" (6:43) evokes the Twelve tribes of Israel. But the second feeding takes place, according to Mark, in Decapolis (see 7:31), that is, in largely pagan territory; thus, those who benefit from the miracle are Gentiles. Following on the Jews, the Gentiles, too, are called to share in the feeding, a pre-figuration of the eucharistic meal and the messianic banquet.

Feeding of the Five Thousand— in Israel (6:31–44)

The details of 6:31–32 are quite vague and the destination is unknown. It is somewhere on the western shore of the Lake—Jewish territory. In the story the loaves are central. Jesus took, blessed, broke, and gave: this is liturgical eucharistic language (see 14: 22). At the close, the disciples gathered *klasmata* (broken pieces of bread); in the early church the term was used of the eucharistic bread. "Twelve baskets": the number twelve evokes the number of the tribes of Israel. And the Greek word *cophinos* was a specifically Jewish word for basket.

In 6:43–44, five thousand had been fed and twelve baskets of the fragments of the bread and fish were collected. In 8:8–9, four thousand were fed and seven baskets of fragments were collected. The differences are obvious, but Mark has given a pointer as to which are, for him, the significant variants: the baskets of fragments. The unexpected emphasis on the baskets of fragments in 8:19–20 is a further indication that this is just where we must look. For there is no denying that Mark does strikingly draw attention to the two feeding stories, deliberately repeating the numbers *twelve* and *seven* and using again (see 6:43; 8:8) two different words for basket: *cophinos*, a basket commonly used by Jews, and *spyris*, an ordinary basket. "Twelve" points to Israel, while the more universal "seven" refers to the Gentiles. Besides, he has insinuated that the first feeding is in a Jewish setting, the other in a Gentile setting (see 7:31). Mark is no careless writer. These details are meaningful for him and, in the setting of this section of his Gospel (6:35—8:26), we are justified in seeing in them deliberate pointers to Jewish and Gentile components of his Christian community. Those of Gentile background as well as those of Jewish origin are both at home in the household of the faith. And this fellowship is achieved in the breaking of the bread.

Lake Crossing

An intriguing feature in Mark is the recurring phrase *eis to peran*, "to the other side," referring to voyages across the Lake of Galilee. While at first sight it may bewilder, a closer look will reveal a clever strategy. It will help to outline the pattern.

At 4:35 we have the beginning of a series of "voyages" to and from the western (Jewish) side of the lake [W] to the eastern (Gentile) side [E]:

4:35	Across to the other side: *eis to peran*	E
5:1	Came to the other side	E
5:21	To the other side	W
[6:32	To a deserted place]	(W)
6:45	To the other side (Bethsaida)	E
6:53	Crossed over (to Gennesaret)	W
7:31	Land journey to Decapolis	E
8:10	Boat journey to Dalmanutha	W
8:13	To the other side (Bethsaida 8:22)	E
8:27	Caesarea Philippi	N
9:30	Galilee (Capernaum)	W

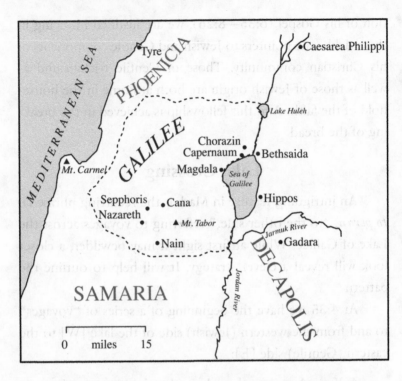

Mark has Jesus crisscrossing the lake: Jewish to Gentile shore, and back and forth. It is a symbolic knitting together of Jew and Gentile, which is achieved in the fellowship of a sharing in the "one loaf" (8:14).

DIVINE PURPOSE

God in the Story

At the baptism of Jesus, the heavens were "torn apart," rent apart by God, as the Spirit, the power of God descended to rest on him. The divine voice declared of Jesus: "You are my Son, the Beloved." From the start, God is, invisibly but actively, present in Mark's story. As Jesus was about to embark on his mission, God solemnly approved both his status and his call. Similarly, at the transfiguration (9:2–13) God declared, "This is my Son, the beloved; listen to him" (9:7). And not only did God, each time, declare that Jesus was "Son," but the declaration served the purpose of confirmation. The baptism declaration confirmed the truth of the opening verse of the Gospel (1:1). The transfiguration declaration confirmed the truth of Peter's confession of Jesus as the "Messiah" (8:29).

In 9:2–13, Jesus led the three disciples Peter, James, and John "up a high mountain" where he was transfigured "before them." Elijah and Moses appeared "to them," and it was for the disciples' benefit that the heavenly voice was heard, speaking of Jesus in the third person (9:7). "It is good for us to be here" (verse 5)—that is to say, this is a happy moment that deserves to be prolonged indefinitely. Wholly forgotten is the word of the suffering and death of the Son of Man (8:31). Peter really "did not know what to say"; he has, once again, totally misunderstood. The voice from heaven sets the record straight: "This is my Son, the Beloved." In contrast to 1:11 (the baptism), the words are here addressed to the disciples (instead of to Jesus): they hear the divine approbation of Jesus as the messianic Son. Suddenly, Elijah and Moses had disappeared and Jesus stood alone. "Listen to him": the Beloved Son, whose love for Father and humankind will be proved in suffering and death, is the revealer of the true God.

At the death of Jesus God intervenes in the story again in the tearing apart of the curtain of the temple (15:38). At the beginning of the story the heavens were rent apart (1:10). Now, at Jesus' death, the veil of the sanctuary is rent asunder. The God who had been, invisibly, in the story throughout will speak his final, decisive word. He will wholly vindicate his Son. This is better treated below.

The whole Jesus story is directed by God, the loving Father. This becomes more apparent as the story moves toward its climax. Mark has carefully signaled the fact.

Paradidomi

The verb *paradidomi* is notably present in the second half of the Gospel. It means to "deliver up," "betray," or "arrest." It occurs twice in the first half. It is a highly significant term, with overtones of divine purpose.

The key to its meaning in Mark is in Acts 2:23. Peter is addressing the Jews: "This Jesus delivered up [*exdidomi*] according to the definite plan and foreknowledge of God, you crucified and killed by the hands of lawless men." This does not mean some cold, inflexible plan. It is, rather, a way of insisting that, strange though it might seem, there is a divine purpose to this tragic drama. A list of the occurrences of the verb will illustrate how pervasive it is:

1:14   After John was arrested [delivered up]

3:19   And Judas Iscariot who betrayed him
       [delivered him up]

9:31   The Son of man will be delivered into the hands of men

10:33 The Son of man will be delivered to the chief priests

13:9   They will deliver you up

13:11 When they bring you to trial and deliver you up

13:12 Brother will deliver up brother to death

14:10 Judas Iscariot went to the chief priests in order to betray him [deliver him up] to them

14:11 He sought an opportunity to betray him [deliver him up]

14:18 one of you will betray me [deliver me up]

14:21 Woe to that man by whom the Son of man is betrayed [delivered up]

14:41 The Son of man is betrayed [delivered up] into the hands of sinners

14:44 Now the betrayer [deliverer up] had given them a sign

14:42 Behold my betrayer [the one who will deliver me up] is at hand

15:1   And delivered him to Pilate

15:10 He perceived that it was out of envy that the chief priests had delivered him up

15:15 Having scourged Jesus, he delivered him up to be crucified

Mark's first summary statement (1:14–15) opens the mission of Jesus and covers its initial stage. The opening words, however, are ominous: "After John was arrested" (literally, "delivered up"). The long shadow of the cross has reached to the start of the Gospel. When we reach the second half—the journey to the cross—the tension is heightened. Beginning with 9:31 ("The Son of Man will be delivered into the hands of men") the emphasis becomes relentless as the occurrences of "deliver up" pile up. At the close is the fatal decision: "Having scourged Jesus, he [Pilate] delivered him up to be crucified." At Gethsemane, Jesus had prayed: "Abba, Father...remove this cup from me; yet, not what I want, but what you want" (14:36). The obedient Son cried out to the Father and put himself wholly in the hands of the Father. Mark has stressed that the suffering and death of Jesus bore the stamp of a loving Father's purpose. That purpose, wholly embraced by the Son, was the salvation of humankind.

On the Way

The central importance of Peter's confession—"You are the Messiah" (8:27–30)—in Mark's editorial structure is indicated by the brusque change of tone and of orientation after Peter has acknowledged the messiahship of Jesus. In the actual structure of the Gospel, the prediction of the passion (8:31–32a) is Jesus' response to the confession of Peter. The following section of the Gospel is dominated by the prophecies of the passion (8:31; 9:31; 10:33–34), each of which is set in a different geographical locale: Caesarea Philippi (8:27), Galilee (9:30), and on the way to Jerusalem (10:32). "Then he began to teach them that the Son of man must undergo great suffering...and be killed" (8:31). The violent protestation of Peter in 8:32 shows clearly that this is a new and unexpected teaching. "He said all this quite openly" (verse 32); it is indeed a turning point in the self-revelation of Jesus: until now he had said nothing explicitly about his messiahship. If he still charges his disciples not to reveal his messianic identity (verse 30)—because their understanding of him is still so imperfect—he now speaks to them quite plainly of his destiny of suffering and death. For, in Mark's intention, 8:31 becomes the starting point of the way of Jesus which ends in Jerusalem with the women at the tomb (16:1–8).

This journey (10:32–34) is headed for a clash in Jerusalem with "the chief priests, the scribes, and the elders" (11:27–33). "Jesus was walking ahead of them" (10:32). He knew where he was going and what fate awaited him in the city. Luke (9:51) has put it aptly: "When the days drew near for him to be taken up, he set his face to go to Jerusalem." The resolute bearing of Jesus as he led the way stirred the disciples with amazement and a sense of foreboding, but they still followed him. As for Jesus himself, perhaps again, Luke has put his finger on Mark's intent: "I must be on my way, because it is impossible for a prophet to be killed outside of Jerusalem" (Luke 13:33). This is the equivalent of "it is written." There is a divine purpose to be fulfilled.

In 10:46, Jesus and his disciples are well on their road to Jerusalem. The narrative of 10:46–52 focuses on the blind beggar Bartimaeus, who is presented as a model of faith in Jesus in spite of discouragement, and as one who eagerly answered the call of the Master and followed him on the way of discipleship. His sight restored, Bartimaeus "followed him on the way" (verse 52). This could mean that the man joined the crowd on their way to Jerusalem. But Jesus had opened his eyes to a deeper reality. There can be no doubt what Mark intends: he followed him on the way of Christian discipleship. The phrase "on the way" and the following of Jesus form an inclusion with verse 32: "They were on the road, going up to Jerusalem, and Jesus was walking ahead of them; they were amazed, and those who followed him were afraid." Only one of faith, enlightened by Jesus, one like Bartimaeus, can walk the way of Jesus without consternation and without fear.

Time Indications through the Passion

A feature of Mark's passion narrative that might very easily be overlooked is his care to mark the passage of time:

14:1   It was two days before the Passover/Unleavened Bread

14:12 On the first day of Unleavened Bread

15:1   As soon as it was morning

15:25 It was nine o'clock in the morning when they crucified him

15:33 When it was noon darkness came over the whole land until three in the afternoon

15:34 At three o'clock Jesus cried out with a loud voice...Then Jesus gave a loud cry and breathed his last

The evangelist marks the passion ordeal of Jesus in three-hourly intervals (15:25, 33, 34). For that matter, precise statements of time, just indicated, are distinctive of the trial and passion narrative. This is to indicate that the passage of time was in accord with the will of God. Nothing at all has happened by chance or unexpectedly.

The way of Jesus had led to the cross and seeming failure. Yet, divinely guided as it was, it could not end in failure—nor did it.

Vindication

By contrast to the mocking challenges hurled at the dying Jesus (15:29–32), there is an emphatically positive response to Jesus' death. The Roman centurion in charge of the execution stood facing a helpless victim on a cross and watched him as he died. In awe, he declared, "Truly, this man was God's Son!" (verse 39). His declaration is to be seen in the immediate context of the rending of the temple curtain from top to bottom (verse 38). The temple had lost its significance (see 11:12–25; 13:2; 14:5–8). It was the end of the cult through which God had hitherto mediated forgiveness of sin and salvation.

Mark's theological point is that a Jesus who had known the pang of God-forsakenness was now wholly vindicated. The temple curtain "was torn"—by God! Salvation is henceforth mediated uniquely through the shedding of his blood by the wholly faithful Son of God. Jesus had already proclaimed as much. He had done so in his words to his disciples: "For the Son of man came not to be served, but to serve, and to give his life as a ransom for many [all]" (14:24). The temple is gone. God's Son is henceforth the "place" of salvation. The chief priests had demanded, in mockery: "Let the Messiah, the King of Israel, come down from the cross now, so that we may see and believe" (verse 32). Now, a Gentile saw and believed. It is the clincher to Mark's theological stance that the revelation of God's Son took place on the cross.

CHAPTER 3

THE ENDING OF MARK'S GOSPEL
The Epilogue (16:1–8)

1. When the Sabbath was over, Mary Magdalene, and Mary the mother of James, and Salome bought spices, so that they might go and anoint him. 2. And very early on the first day of the week, when the sun had risen, they went to the tomb. 3. They had been saying to one another, "Who will roll away the stone for us from the entrance to the tomb?" 4. When they looked up, they saw that the stone, which was very large, had already been rolled back. 5. As they entered the tomb, they saw a young man, dressed in a white robe, sitting on the right side; and they were alarmed. 6. But he said to them, "Do not be alarmed; you are looking for Jesus of Nazareth, who was crucified. He has been

raised; he is not here. Look, there is the place where they laid him. 7. But go, tell his disciples and Peter that he is going ahead of you to Galilee: there you will see him, just as he told you." 8. So they went out and fled from the tomb, for terror and amazement had seized them; *and they said nothing to anyone, for they were afraid.*

Mark relates that the three women named in 15:40 and 47 who had witnessed the death and burial of Jesus bought spices when the Sabbath had ended (after 6:00 P.M.). Their purpose is in step with the hasty burial (15:46). The large stone that sheltered the body would have presented a problem. To their surprise, they found that the stone "had already been rolled back." This is the "divine passive": God had acted!

The "young man" dressed in white is an angel. Their awe and his words of assurance are stock features of such angelic visitations. They had come seeking Jesus; they had seen where his body had been laid. Again they look upon the spot, but he is no longer there. The "young man" plays the role of *angelus interpres*, a feature of apocalyptic. They were faced with the riddle of an empty tomb: he explains why the tomb is empty. It is a neat literary way of presenting, as briefly as possible, the fact of the empty tomb and the real explanation of its emptiness.

The women had sought Jesus of Nazareth: an important title for Mark. He has used it from the beginning (1:9, 24) and stresses it again at the end (14:67; 16:6), a reminder that Jesus is the man of Galilee. And he is "the crucified one," practically a title as well. "He has been raised": the answer to the cry of God-forsakenness (15:34). Jesus has not been forsaken! Apparent failure has been transformed into victory—by God. The women were given a message, the echo of a promise made by Jesus on the way to Gethsemane (14:28), a message for the disciples and especially for Peter. Jesus is going before them into Galilee; they will see him there.

The men disciples of Jesus had abandoned him and fled for their lives (14:50). The women disciples did not lose heart: they followed him as far as women might, looking on the crucifixion scene "from afar" (15:40). Mark names three of the group; the impression is of a relatively large group. They were Galileans who had "followed" Jesus and had "come up with him" to Jerusalem—again discipleship. It is because they had continued to follow him, if even "from afar," that the Easter message is entrusted to them. They alone, of all others, had followed to the cross. These women disciples have stood steadfast and have not been ashamed of Jesus (8:38).

But have not the women, too, failed at the end? They were given a message: "Go, tell his disciples and Peter that he is going ahead of you to Galilee" (16:7). But what kind of messengers did they turn out to be? "They said nothing to anyone, for they were afraid *(ephobounto gar)* (verse 8). They, too, experienced the basic ground of discipleship failure: fear.

The other evangelists agree in asserting that the women did, in fact, fulfill their messenger role: Matthew 28:6–10; Luke 24:4–11; John 20:17–18. Evidently, it is a well-established tradition. Mark, however, has consciously painted a different picture. Why has Mark so radically altered a well-known tradition?[1] The key to an answer is found in his consistent focus on the failure of Jesus' disciples. Mark removes all initiative from humans and places it with God—a procedure very much in line with Saint Paul and the Pauline tradition. In the end, all human beings fail. God alone succeeds. The Father had not abandoned the Son (15:34), but had raised Jesus from the dead (16:6). The failed disciples will encounter the risen Lord in Galilee, not because they have succeeded, but solely because of the initiative of God. The account of a reunion with the Risen One promised in 14:28 and again 16:7 is not in the text of Mark's Gospel. The very existence of his story assures us that the meeting had occurred. And it promises that the Lord will be encountered in every Christian community that embraces his Gospel. The ending of the Gospel sees Mark at his most artistic and most profound.

If today we acknowledge that Mark did intend to end his Gospel at 16:8, this was not always so. Even early Christians had been disconcerted by this abrupt closure of the Gospel. A second-century author decided to round off Mark's work—with our 16:9–20. Although rather widely attested, the fact remains that, in the older Greek manuscripts of Mark and in important manuscripts of early versions, this passage does not appear. The vocabulary and style of the passage show that it was not written by Mark. It is based on knowledge of the traditions found in the other Gospels and Acts. The author of the "Longer Ending" did achieve his purpose. He resolved the enigmatic ending of 16:8, continued the Gospel themes of failure of the disciples and mission, and filled out the brief reference to resurrection in 16:6 with appearances of the risen Jesus. But he has blunted the stark message of Mark.

What has been set out in Part I should demonstrate that Mark is, indeed, a creative and skillful writer. His book is carefully crafted. He has consistently nudged the reader to look where he wants the reader to look. His concern is that his message be discerned and grasped. It is to this message that we now turn our attention.

PART TWO

THE

MESSAGE

THE

MESSAGE

CHAPTER 4

THE CHRIST

We have seen something of Mark's literary sophistication. That skill of his was geared to the effective presentation of his message. He presents the Good News in terms of Christology (the theological understanding of Jesus) and discipleship. Jesus—*Christos*/Messiah—is, of course, the focus of his concern. He views this Jesus as Prophet, Teacher, Healer, and Son of God. He is the suffering Messiah, this Son of God "who loved me, and gave himself for me" (Galatians 2:20). We know him in the paradox of the cross, that proclamation of *divine* love. Discipleship of a crucified Messiah is a challenge. Mark does not draw a veil over its demands. Always it is the gracious God of infinite love who reveals his true self in that cross.

PROPHET

In the biblical context a prophet is God's spokesperson: one called and sent to proclaim the word of God. Old Testament prophets were very conscious of the call and of the task. We see this already when we look at an Amos, a Hosea, an Isaiah, a Jeremiah. "The Lord took me from following the flock...and the Lord said to me, 'Go, prophesy to my people Israel'" (Amos 7:15). "Then I heard the voice of the Lord saying, 'Whom shall I send?'...And I said, 'Here am I, send me'" (Isaiah 6:8). "Before I formed you in the womb I knew you...I appointed you a prophet to the nations" (Jeremiah 1:5). The call was a powerful summons; the task was challenging and formidable. There was need for commitment and courage. By and large, the prophetic word would not be heard. The task involved suffering and rejection—even death. Jeremiah is a poignant instance of the loneliness of the call: "Under the weight of your hand I sat alone" (Jeremiah 15:17). The mysterious prophetical figure of Second Isaiah paid the price in vicarious suffering: "He was despised and rejected. He was wounded for our transgressions...it was the will of the Lord to crush him with pain...yet he bore the sin of many and made intercession for the transgressors" (Isaiah 53:3–12).

John the Baptist was a prophet in the stern line of Amos, an eschatological prophet who looked to an imminent end and judgment—and the definitive salvation of the just. He paid the ultimate price for his fidelity to the word. Jesus of Nazareth, a one-time disciple of John,[1] was a prophet who shared something of the eschatological expectation of the Baptist. In significant ways he differed from John. Christians saw him as "the more powerful one" spoken of by the Baptist. He, too, was rejected and put to death.

It would be well to clear up any potential misunderstanding of the terms *prophet* and *prophecy*. In current language they

carry the exclusive meaning of prediction. This is not at all the
primary sense of biblical usage. A biblical prophet—the
spokesperson of God—addressed, first and foremost, the contemporary situation. He tended to be an outspoken critic of
the religious and political status quo. He was proclaimer of
God's purpose for his people. A text in the Acts of the Apostles
may be adapted to characterize the prophetic style. The little
Christian group is shown at prayer. They besought the Lord to
"grant your servants to speak your word with all boldness"
(Acts 4:29). Their prayer was answered: "They were all filled
with the Holy Spirit and spoke the word of God with boldness" (4:31). A prophet, in word or deed, proclaimed the
word of God with boldness. This did involve concern for the
future. There was prediction, in its measure, but always in relation to the current situation. Any reference to the future had
meaning and relevance for the prophet's audience.

The prophet was convinced that the message of Jesus,
lived and spoken, was of utmost urgency. Here we look to the
prophet Jesus as perceived by the Christian eyes of Mark. If
Jesus was prophet, he was also much else. Or perhaps one
might put it that other features of his activity were facets of his
prophetic role. At any rate, he emerges as teacher and healer,
and to be seen as Messiah and Son of God. He was surely the
Suffering Servant.

Proclamation

After John had been arrested [delivered up] Jesus
came to Galilee, proclaiming the good news of God
and saying, "The time is fulfilled, and the kingdom

of God has come near; repent, and believe in the good news." (Mark 1:14–15)

Mark's first summary statement (see chapter 2) opens the public ministry of Jesus and covers its initial phase. The opening words are ominous: "After John was arrested [delivered up]." The fate of the Baptist was to be delivered up to his enemies (6:17–29) "according to the definite plan and foreknowledge of God" (see Acts 2:23), that is, after a mysterious divine purpose. The Baptist was a type of the suffering Messiah (see Mark 9:11–13); the long shadow of the cross reaches to the start of the Gospel. Yet now began the preaching of the "good news of peace," and Mark's sentence "the kingdom [rule] of God has come near; repent and believe in the good news" is an admirable summing-up of the preaching and message of Jesus. Like the Baptist (Mark 1:4), Jesus called for thoroughgoing conversion. More urgently, he called on people to embrace the good news. The evangelist intended the words "believe in the good news" to be taken in the sense of faith in the good news of salvation through Jesus Christ.

Jesus is here firmly cast as a prophet, issuing a challenge and an invitation. He had a burning desire for the renewal of the people of Israel as God's holy elect. He would not define the holiness of God's people in cultic terms. He redefined it in terms of wholeness. Where other contemporary Jewish groups were, in their various ways, exclusive, the Jesus movement was inclusive. His challenge and his invitation were to all. What Jesus claimed was that the decisive intervention of God expected in the end time was, in some sort, happening in his ministry. The kingdom is here and now present in history in that the power of evil spirits is broken, sins are forgiven, and sinners are gathered into God's friendship. The kingdom, though in its fullness still in the future, comes as a present offer, in actual gift, through the proclamation of the good news. But it arrives only on condition of the positive response of the hearer.

The Kingdom of God

The precise phrase *kingdom of God* occurs only once in the Old Testament, in Wisdom 10:10. The expression was not current in Judaism at the time of Jesus and was not widely used by early Christians. "Kingdom of God" is found predominantly in the Synoptic Gospels and then almost always on the lips of Jesus. It was evidently central to Jesus' proclamation. Israel regarded God as universal king. And there was the expectation that God's reign would soon be manifested over the whole world. This is why "reign" or "rule" of God is a more satisfactory rendering of the Aramaic *malkutha di' elaha*—the language of Jesus.

Jesus spoke, in the main, of a future kingdom. In the Lord's Prayer, he taught his disciples to pray that God's kingdom come—that God would come at the end to save his people (Matt 6:10; Luke 11:2). In Matthew 8:11–12 (Luke 13:28–29), Jesus spoke of many coming from east and west (Gentiles) to join Abraham, Isaac, and Jacob at the glorious banquet in the kingdom of God. In Mark 14:25 (Luke 22:18), Jesus, in prophesying his imminent death, confidently saw himself at that banquet—drinking new wine in the kingdom of God.

And the beatitudes, in their Q form (see Luke 6:20–21; Q is the hypothetical common source of Matthew and Luke in which they differ from Mark, their basic source), have as their background God as vindicator of widows and orphans, as champion of the oppressed.

There is evidence that Jesus also spoke of the kingdom as in some fashion already present in his own words and deeds. When we have in mind the fact that "kingdom of God" is not primarily a state or place, but rather the dynamic event of God coming in power to rule his people Israel in the end time, it is not surprising that the precise relationship between a future and a present kingdom is not specified. That is why Jesus can speak of the kingdom as both imminent and yet present. In Jesus' eyes, his healings and exorcisms were part of the eschatological drama that was being already played out and on which God was about to bring down the curtain. The important point is that Jesus deliberately chose to proclaim that the display of miraculous power throughout his ministry was a preliminary and partial realization of God's kingly rule.

Gesture

In the style of Old Testament prophets, the prophet Jesus, too, performed prophetic gestures, designed to bolster the prophetic word. For Mark's readers the coming of Jesus to Jerusalem (11:1–11) had an evident messianic significance. It is likely that the episode happened not at Passover but at a feast of Dedication (*Hanukhah*), and Mark's narrative suggests that it was a modest affair: the immediate disciples and Jesus riding in their midst. Nothing would have been more commonplace than a man riding a donkey, and a small group of pilgrims, waving branches and shouting acclamations from Psalm 118, would not have occasioned a second glance at the feast of Dedication. Yet whatever others might have thought, those who could see (certainly, Christian readers of the Gospels) perceive that this entry to Jerusalem, as it is here presented, was the solemn entry of the Savior-King into his city. Jesus himself took the initiative: he would enter as the King of Zechariah 9:9, where it is Yahweh, as a divine warrior, who rides into Jerusalem. In Mark there is a studied reticence. The text of Zechariah 9:9 is not quoted (see Matthew 21:5); there are no "crowds" (Matthew 21:9) or "multitude" (Luke 19:37, 39); the people had not actually proclaimed Jesus as "Son of David" (see Matthew 21:9), though they had spread their cloaks and leafy branches for his passage. In this entry to Jerusalem Jesus himself, for the first time in the Gospel, made a messianic gesture—but in a special manner, wholly in keeping with his destiny of one who had come to serve and to lay down his life.

Despite the "many" of 11:8, Mark does not give the impression that the accompanying crowd was large, yet they walked before and after Jesus, forming a procession. The entry, as depicted in Mark, meant the coming of a Messiah who was poor, an advent in humility, not in glory. What was at stake for Jesus was the nature and manner of his messiahship. At this moment, come to the city that would so soon witness his passion and death, he could manifest himself. But he did not come as a temporal ruler or with worldly pomp. He came as a religious figure (in his distinctive understanding of religion), a prince of peace, "humble and riding on a donkey" (Zechariah 9:9). Inevitably, he was misunderstood. "Blessed is the coming kingdom of our father David!": his followers voiced their expectation that he would restore the kingdom of David. Jesus turned from the acclamation. He entered the temple by himself, unobserved; the procession seems to have petered out before the actual entry. His "looking around" involved a critical scrutiny that set the stage for the next episode.

The prophetic gesture of Jesus, his "cleansing" of the temple (11:15–19), symbolically disrupted the temple's cultic life. He is depicted as driving out those who offered for sale animals and birds and other commodities needed for the sacrifices, the pilgrims who bought from them, and the money changers who changed the Greek and Roman currency of the pilgrims into the Jewish or Tyrian coinage in which alone the temple tax could be paid. He prohibited the carrying of cultic vessels. It is inconceivable, particularly so near Passover with its influx of pilgrims, that Jesus could really have cleared the crowded temple courts and brought the whole elaborate business to a standstill. His action, on a necessarily very limited scale, was a prophetic gesture, and would have been recognized as such (verse 18).

The motivation of his action is given in verse 17. It opens with Markan emphasis on the teaching of Jesus and runs into a quotation of Isaiah 56:7, with an echo of Jeremiah 7:11. It was God's intention that the temple should be a house of prayer "for all nations"—of special interest to Mark. This had not been achieved because the temple remained the jealously guarded preserve of Israel. Worse, the temple and its cult had become a "den of robbers," as Jeremiah 7:8–11 makes plain. The temple and its service had become an escape hatch: the temple cult, it was felt, would automatically win forgiveness of ill behavior and bring about communion with God. The prophet Jesus was, in this respect, emphatically in the line of Amos, Hosea, and Jeremiah (see Amos 4:4–5; 5:21–24; Hosea 5:1–2; 6:1–6; Jeremiah 7:1–15; 26:1–19). In his view, however, because it was so abused, the temple cult had no longer any raison d'etre. Its time had run out. The prophetic gesture presaged what his death was to achieve (Mark 15:38; see 13:2; 14:58; 15:29). The chief priests and the scribes heard the message (see 11:28). They would not forget; they bided their time. One might observe that with the inclusion of the theme of prayer (11:22–25), Mark makes the point that, for Jesus' disciples, prayer takes the place of temple worship and marks a turn from places and practices that are no longer authentic.

A Prophet without Honor

The episode of the rejection of Jesus at Nazareth (6:1–6a) had deep meaning for Mark and he set it deliberately at this point in his Gospel. A poignant problem in the early days of the church was the fact that while many Gentiles were responding to the good news, the Jewish people resisted it (see Romans 9—11).

Already, in Mark, the bitter opposition of the authorities to Jesus has been demonstrated (2:1— 3:6). Now, at the close of the Galilean ministry, his own townspeople were challenged to make up their minds about his person and his claims, and they took offense at him. Their rejection of him was an antic-ipation of his rejection by the Jewish nation (15:11–15). That final rejection was possible because the blindness of God's people to God's revelation had been present from the start (see John 1:10–11). The issue is one of faith or unfaith in Jesus—or, in Christian terms, faith in or rejection of the Lord.

The passage lays bare one of the roots of unbelief. Jesus' townsfolk reacted with initial surprise. They wondered at the origin ("where") of his wisdom; they had heard of his "deeds of power." But they made the mistake of imagining that they already had the answers to their own questions. Besides, there was the scandal of Jesus' ordinariness: they could not bring themselves to acknowledge the greatness or the mission of a man who was one of themselves. "He could do no deed of power there": Jesus' healings were always in an atmosphere of faith; there was no context of faith in his hometown. The healing of a few sick people (verse 5) is evidently not regarded as miraculous.

They "took offense" at him: by Mark's day, *skandalon* had practically become a technical term to designate the obstacle that some found in Christ and that blocked them from passing to Christian faith and discipleship (see Romans 9:32–33; 1 Corinthians 1:23; 1 Peter 2:8). The proverb of Mark 6:4 ("Prophets are not without honor, except in their hometown") in some form was current in the ancient world. Jesus implicitly assumed the role of prophet. His word must have consoled the early church in face of the enigmatic refusal of the chosen people as a whole to accept the message of Jesus. Christian communities down the centuries would have done well to have taken it to heart. Prophets are never comfortable people to have about and we are adept at finding ways of discrediting them.

Rejection

"Jerusalem, Jerusalem, the city that kills the prophets, and stones those who are sent to it" (Luke 13:34; Matthew 23:37). It is the fate of a prophet to find oneself ignored, rejected, or worse. Jesus was no exception and, as we have seen, was conscious of it. Jesus had carried out his mission in Galilee: teaching, healing, and exorcizing (Mark 1). Soon there was confrontation, documented in a series of five controversies (2:1—3:6). The series closes on a rather sinister note: "The Pharisees went out and immediately conspired with the Herodians against him, how to destroy him" (3:6). The odd association of Pharisees and Herodians (supporters of Herod Antipas) may be explained by the link between the Baptist and Jesus. The typical opponents of Jesus (Pharisees) joined with the supporters of the man who had had John executed in a common plot to have Jesus put to death. Now we know that the hostility of the religious authorities—it was the Jerusalem priests who brought about the death of Jesus, but "Pharisees" will serve as the opponents—can have no other issue. Death, in Mark's story, looms as a dark cloud over the future course of Jesus' ministry.

The Beloved Son

The allegorical features of the parable of the Wicked Tenants (12:1–12) are evident: the vineyard is Israel, the owner is God, the maltreated servants are God's messengers to Israel, notably the prophets, and the beloved son is Jesus. "Then he began to speak to them in parables" (verse 1); "they" are the chief priests, scribes, and elders (see 11:27; 12:12). The Old Testament has a notable instance of a prophet employing a parable with dramatic effect: Nathan's entrapment of David (2 Samuel 12:1–7). Mark's parable, too, is dramatic. The description and equipping of the vineyard (Mark 12:1) are based on the allegory found in Isaiah 5:1–7, which represents Israel as Vineyard of the Lord. Mark's significant modification is to have the landlord let out his vineyard to tenants. It follows that failure is not on the part of the vineyard (the people) as in Isaiah; the failure is of the tenants, the leaders of the people. And, in its Gospel setting, the vineyard is no longer Israel but the broader reality of the kingdom.

The landlord sent his servants to collect his rent, only to have them insulted, maltreated, and even killed. He decided to play his last card. He had a beloved son, his only son. He would send him: "Surely, they will respect my son!" But they killed him and, contemptuously, left him unburied (verses 6–8). So had God dealt with an obdurate people, sending to them, time and again, his servants the prophets. And now, with supreme graciousness, he has sent his only Son. This was the ultimate challenge. But the tenants, the leaders, did away with him. Jesus' rhetorical question in verse 9 ("What will the owner of the vineyard do?") gives punch to the parable; his reply points to judgment on faithless Israel. The tenants, the leaders of the covenant people, have brought upon themselves their own dismissal; they have rejected the Son of God (verse 9). God looks to others. Mark, likely, has Gentiles in mind. The parable is aptly in place after 11:12–21 (prophetic gestures aimed at the temple) and after the question about Jesus' authority (11:27–33). And when there is question of the alleged rejection of Israel, one must keep in mind the conviction of Paul who, after all, as a fellow Jew, had close affinity with Jesus of Nazareth, that "all Israel will be saved" (Romans 1:26). Why? On the basis of impeccable biblical argument: "The gifts and the calling of God are irrevocable" (11:29). It is a matter of supreme importance that this parable appears in all three Synoptic Gospels shortly before their passion narratives. It is a wholly clear indication of how the evangelists understood "He did not spare his own Son." The Father had not thrown his Son to the wolves. The Father had not wished the death of his Son. Father and Son had delivered themselves to the humans they would save. Jesus did not die—he was killed. But it was not the Father who killed Jesus.

With the question of Psalm 118:22–23 in mind, in verses 10–11 the figure passes from vineyard to that of building: God's rejected Son has become the cornerstone, the foundation, of the new community. Mark's readers can take heart; they are stones in a building raised by God himself (see Ephesians 2:19–22). In his conclusion (verse 12), Mark typically distinguished between the hostile teachers of Israel and the common people who were sympathetic to Jesus (see 11:18). The leaders had caught the drift of the parable only too well (verse 12): "When they realized that he had told this parable against them, they wanted to arrest him, but they feared the crowd." They remained "those outside" (4:11) because they rejected its challenge. They could not bring themselves to acknowledge Jesus. They had rejected the prophet; now they must silence him.

Summary

Jesus of Nazareth had responded to the challenge of the uncompromising prophet: John the Baptist. He became a prophet in his turn and began to proclaim the good news of the rule of God. Soon God would come in power, bringing about the great reversal, but one did not wait passively for it to happen. There must be human openness and human response. Besides, the rule of God was already present—present in Jesus, in his words and deeds. It could not be otherwise: in Jesus, God was present and active. Besides, he, as prophet, had been sent. After remarkable success at Capernaum (1:21–34), Jesus had gone to pray (1:35) and Simon and his companions "hunted for him" (1:36). They felt that he, wonder-worker and healer (verses 32–34), was missing a great opportunity. Jesus would not be turned from his prophetic task of proclaiming the kingdom of God (1:14). "For that is what I came out to do" (verse 38): he explained to his disciples that he must not linger to satisfy the curiosity of the people of Capernaum. Luke had correctly caught the Markan nuance when he wrote: "for I was sent for this purpose" (Luke 4:43), that is, sent by the Father. The kernel of his prophetic message was that the kingdom of God had come near.

God's rule becomes real only when it finds expression in human life. It found expression in the life of Jesus. He "went about, doing good"; he championed the outcast and welcomed sinners. Jesus, in his own lifestyle, gave concrete expression to the good life—a life worthy of humankind. It is up to us, his disciples, in our different and greatly changed world, to give expression, in our terms, to the good life. It is our task to give the kingdom flesh and blood in our world. Of course, the kingdom that would emerge if God's rule were to hold sway would be very different from any political entity and different, too, from any religious structure, then and since.

The kingdom can be a reality only at the cost of wholehearted conversion. It is the charism of a prophet to see to the heart of things. Only the starkest words can match his uncomplicated vision. The genuine prophet will speak a message of comfort, based on the faithfulness of God, but it will never be a comfortable message. That is why Jesus' demands were uncompromising. He knew, better than any other, that sin was the greatest evil, the ultimate slavery. He discerned sin in selfishness and greed, in the seeking of status—most reprehensively in the seeking of ecclesiastical power and privilege. Indeed, he turned authority upside down (see Mark 10:42–45). He took his stand on the Fatherhood/Motherhood of God. He believed that all men and women are children of this Parent, that all are sisters and brothers. He regarded sin as whatever conflicts with that family relationship of respect and love. Logically, then, his prophetic message was "good news for the poor." The poor were victims of the oppressive power of sin, an oppression mediated through sinful structures. This concern of the Old Testament prophets found fresh urgency in Jesus' preaching.

In preaching the rule of God, Jesus was defining God. That is why he announced good news to the poor—the needy of every sort, the outcast. That is why he was a friend of sinners, why he had table fellowship with them. And, in the long run, it was because Jesus had proclaimed a God of overwhelming mercy that he ended up on a cross. That God was unacceptable to the religious people of his day. That God is unacceptable to the "professional" religious of any day.

Jesus was aware of the fate of prophets; he suffered the fate of a prophet, that is, he was rejected and put to death. By the standard of the world he was a failure. True, he had got off to a promising start in his acknowledged task of renewing Israel and he had evoked a heartening response. But opposition began to emerge almost from the start. As Peter showed at Caesarea Philippi, those who began to pin vague or explicit messianic expectations on him quickly became disillusioned: what was all this about suffering and death? (see Mark 8:27–33). The poignant words of the Emmaus disciples are eloquent: "We had hoped that he was the one to redeem Israel!" (Luke 24:21). They had been left down with a bang.

Failure is an unavoidable factor of our human existence. While there is failure that is blameworthy, there is much failure beyond our control. Surely, it would be comfort, in our season of failure, to know that Jesus, too, like Jeremiah, had had a real experience of failure. We recall the consoling words of Hebrews: "Because he himself was tested by what he suffered, he is able to help those who are being tested" (Hebrews 2:18). Surely, it is heartening, in the dejection of failure, to hear in the silence of prayer, the gentle, reassuring words: "My sister, my brother, I, too, knew the agony of failure." To hear these words we must first be prepared to acknowledge a Jesus who could suffer a sense of failure. If our Christology will not allow for that, then he can be no comfort to us in our times of failure. The Christology of Mark allows for it. The Jesus of Mark's Gospel, as prophet sent by God, fulfilled the role of the Servant (Isaiah 52:1—53:12). We need to know the Jesus of Mark and the ultimate promise of the cross: the triumph of failure. In Jesus, God's victory has been won on the cross. Hence, the Christian paradox: the victim is the victor (see Revelation 5:6, 9, 12).

TEACHER

While Mark gives, in comparison with Matthew and Luke, little of the *teaching* of Jesus—but more than is regularly acknowledged—he does insist, firmly, on the *teaching activity* of Jesus. If Jesus were, undoubtedly, prophet, he stood, too, in the line of Old Testament wisdom teachers. On the first Sabbath of his ministry, Jesus taught in the Capernaum synagogue (Mark 1:21). Later, in a house, he continued to "speak the word" to the people of the town (2:2) and taught crowds gathered by the lake of Galilee (2:13; 4:1). He taught, this time without success, in his Nazareth synagogue (6:2). At first, however, his hearers spontaneously recognized the significance of his presence: "Where did this man get all this? What is this wisdom that has been given to him?" He was, it must have seemed, purporting to be a wisdom-teacher. And when a great crowd followed him to a desert place, his first concern was that they lacked a teacher. They were like sheep without a shepherd, "and he began to teach them many things" (6:34). His teaching covered a wide range.

In Jesus, the roles of prophet and teacher overlapped— as they regularly did with the prophets of Israel. Jesus taught distinctively. And he taught with authority. As a first-century Palestinian Jew he, of course, shared much of the theology of his tradition. But there was more than enough to set him apart. The ultimate factor was his understanding of God. Clashes with his religious opponents over matters of law, such as Sabbath observance, were symptomatic of fundamental difference. Jesus knew, better than any other, that to proclaim one's belief in God is not enough. What matters, and matters utterly, is the kind of God in whom one believes. It literally makes a world of difference whether one's God is the true God or a distorted image of that God. For Jesus, God is God of humankind. He is found where there is goodness and a striving for the liberation of humankind. We are human beings, created in the image of God; we are meant to image God. Our destiny is to be human—as God understands humanness. The corollary is that only with God can we reach full humanness. Jesus, with God, reached whole humanness.

Here, it is widely believed, is where religion comes in. Religion, generally seen as the area of humankind's relation with God, is ostensibly a system and manner of life that unites us with God and thus enables us to be godly. Like all things human, religion is subject to corruption. The temptation of the religious person is to identify one's human-made world with the world of God and claim control over the holy. In practice, religion may be a barrier to creative union with God; it may lock us into a narrow, impoverished way. Jesus uttered his word, at once criterion and critique: "The sabbath was made for humankind, and not humankind for the sabbath" (Mark 2:27). Decoded, it runs: "Religion is in the service of men and women; men and women are not slaves of religion." Wherever religion is burden, wherever it shows lack of respect for human freedom, it has become an oppressor, not a servant. Authentic religion must foster freedom. Of course, one has to understand freedom correctly. In a Christian context, freedom is never license to do as one pleases. Paradoxically, the ultimate freedom is freedom to serve: "the Son of Man came not to be served but to serve, and to give his life as a ransom for many [all]" (10:45. Here is the sure christological basis of authentic freedom.

Mark has presented Jesus as Teacher and has given an indication of the range of his teaching. One thing emerges unmistakably: Jesus had an eschatological perspective indeed, but he was deeply concerned with life in the here and now. He sought to reform Israel: he desired the fabric of life in his day to be transformed. Jesus had a refreshingly realistic understanding of salvation. Salvation happens in our world, in our history. Salvation comes from God but touches every aspect of human life. Otherwise it would not be salvation of humankind. Salvation is not confined within the limits of religion. Indeed, too often, religion is and has been an obstacle to salvation—the whole liberation of the wholly human. And it is only where men and women are free to be truly human that the human person becomes the image of God. It is only so that the true being of God may be revealed. Being image of God is not only the reflection of God but the revelation of God. Jesus of Nazareth, in Mark's portrait, is the supreme image of God. The Markan Jesus is, transparently, the one "like his brothers and sisters in every respect" who is, at the same time, and in his sheer humanness, "the reflection of God's glory and the exact imprint of God's very being" (Hebrews 2:17; 1:3).

Demanding Teacher

Jesus offers no soft option. Christians may be children of God but only on condition that they understand what this means and live what it demands. The manner of being child of God has been firmly traced: "Anyone who wants to be a follower of mine must renounce self, take up one's cross and follow me" (Mark 8:34). Jesus delivered a challenge, the challenge of his own way as Son. Being a disciple is a serious business. Yet taking up one's cross is not at all to say that suffering is something Christians should seek. Jesus did not seek suffering; Gethsemane is clear enough. But suffering will be part of Christian life as it was part of Jesus' life. The comfort is that the following can be in tiny steps. God is patient. His challenge is invitation. Faithfulness to one's way of life, concern for others in whatever manner, the caring gesture, the kind word— these add up. There will be heroes, the few; there will be those whose way will seem ordinary, drab—the many. Even in the things of God we are prone to measure by worldly standards. The Lord does not overlook the painful decision, the unspoken sorrow, the secret suffering. There are many more saints than those whom we honor as such. It would be wise not to overlook the minor characters of Mark's Gospel.

It Shall Not Be So

In the religious sphere, Jesus could not avoid a clash with the religious authorities of Judaism. He did not set out to challenge, head-on, social and political structures. One should note, however, that his paradoxical view of authority was subversive of authority as domination. One might further maintain that while his attack on "unclean spirits" was, in fact, an attack on disease, his war against "Satan" was war against oppressive and dehumanizing power structures. Jesus always aimed at root causes. It is not surprising, then, that there is no evidence of his having ever taken a specific stand against Roman domination. For that matter, when challenged, he declared, "Give to the emperor the things that are the emperor's, and to God the things that are God's" (12:17). The tenor of his teaching made clear his assumption that Caesar's claim would be just: he did not grant Caesar a blank check. His concern went far deeper than any given political entity. And never would he envisage violence as a way to political and social change. His demand to "Love your enemy" is a radical disavowal of violence. It is a challenge that carries within it the seed of the destruction of violence.

The Authority of Jesus

It is clear from the Gospels that Jesus had *exousia*—authority—from God. It is equally clear that this power of his did not have any shade of domination. Mark does indeed show Jesus having facile authority over evil spirits (the exorcisms) and over nature (the stilling of the tempest). But Jesus' authority did not include lording it over people. For that matter, in relation to people, he was largely helpless. The hallmark of the use of his authority in relation to people was consistently and emphatically that of *diakonia*, service. If Jesus did serve others, it was always from a position of strength. He would not do what others wanted him to do unless it be consonant with God's will. He would lead, but he would not control. He healed, both physically and spiritually, looking for nothing else than openness to his healing touch. He was a friend of sinners, but we must not allow ourselves subconsciously to think that they were repentant before he was their friend. No, he befriended them in their brokenness.

Jesus certainly confronted the religious authorities, but without seeking to impose his authority on them. He was content to hold the mirror up to them, urging them to discern in their attitude and conduct a betrayal of God's rule. But this was the measure of it. Response was their responsibility. Jesus sought no advantage from his authority. He laid claim to no titles; it was up to others to identify him. In his healing ministry Jesus became the man who relieved suffering. At the end he was the vulnerable one who became victim of suffering. He was, after all, the one who had come "to serve, and to give his life as a ransom for many [all]" (Mark 10:45).

In short, Jesus, in his authority, as in all else, mirrored God. For God, the God of infinite power, is never a God of force. The Son never did, nor would he ever, resort to force.

HEALER

Those who are well have no need of a physician, but those who are sick; I have come to call not the righteous but sinners. (Mark 2:17)

Miracles

All four Gospels agree that Jesus worked miracles—and not just a few but many. Miracle has been aptly defined by John Meier:

A miracle is (1) an unusual, startling, or extraordinary event that is in principle perceivable by any interested and fair-minded observer, (2) an event which finds no reasonable explanation in human abilities or in other know forces that operate in our world of time and space, and (3) an event that is the result of a special act of God doing what no human power can do.[2]

Recognition of miracle as such is always a philosophical or theological judgment. It is not possible for historian or exegete, in terms of their disciplines, to judge that God has acted in this or that event in a manner beyond human power. With regard to the Gospel miracles a number of questions need to be asked. Are reports of miracles attributed to Jesus creations of the early church, or can at least some of these reports be traced back to the time and activity of the historical Jesus? Did Jesus, in fact, perform actions acknowledged as miracles by himself and his followers? If so, what did these miracles mean in the context of his ministry?

In the modern world, many find it difficult to accommodate the notion of miracle; many reject the possibility of miracle. In contrast, in the Greco-Roman world of Jesus' day, miracles were quite willingly acknowledged. If Jesus did perform miracles they would readily be accepted as such by his contemporaries. The question is if he did, in fact, perform miracles. Here the familiar criteria of multiple attestation and coherence come into play.[3] The criterion of *multiple attestation* is here twofold: 1) multiple sources—all four Gospels carry accounts of several miracles; 2) multiple literary forms— exorcism stories, healing stories, and accounts of nature miracles. The criterion of *coherence* discerns an impressive convergence of actions and sayings of Jesus; miracle stories do fit into the pattern of his deeds and words. These criteria firmly support the tradition of Jesus' miracles. It is reasonably certain that Jesus did perform startling deeds regarded by himself and others as miracles. Among these were assuredly deeds of healing.

Jesus' reputation as miracle worker is firmly established in the Gospels. The majority of the miracles are healings of varied diseases. This healing activity was not only motivated by his concern for suffering or his sympathy with the afflicted; it was also a sign of the in-breaking of the kingdom. The saving power of God was making its way into the lives of men and women.

Exorcist

If it is by the finger of God that I cast out demons, then the kingdom of God has come to you. (Luke 11:20)

Prominent among Jesus' miraculous deeds—especially so in Mark—were exorcisms. This aspect of Jesus' activity can and does upset our modern sensibility. The situation is aggravated by theatrical exploitation of the subject and by quite harmful interventions of would-be "exorcists." In the world of Jesus, on the other hand, exorcism was readily accepted both in paganism and in Judaism. It is, then, to be expected rather than come as a surprise that Jesus figured as an exorcist and "probably won not a little of his fame and following by practicing exorcisms."[4] In this aspect of Jesus' ministry, above all, we can perceive the difference between the historical Jesus on the one hand and modern Western culture and scientific technology on the other. People in the Mediterranean world of the first century attributed such disorders as epilepsy and what we now term mental illness to demonic possession; medical knowledge was not sufficiently far advanced to do otherwise. Jesus undoubtedly understood the healing and liberating dimensions of his ministry in terms of exorcism. He was a first-century Jew, a man of his own day.

An obvious corollary is that a twenty-first-century Jesus would view the situation very differently. He would not be an exorcist. We must adjust our perspective to a first-century worldview. The exorcisms of Jesus were, in fact, healings. The difference between them and the recognized healings is that in the exorcism the current view that human ills were due to evil forces that warred against us was more pronounced. And in them, too, the apocalyptic dimension was more present—here, more than elsewhere. We face the fact that Jesus of Nazareth was authentically a first-century Jew. When the author of Hebrews declared that Jesus "had to become like his brothers and sisters in every respect" (2:17), he really meant it. Every human is influenced by his or her culture. We are people of our age, no matter how well we may come to understand people of other times and places. We cannot turn the historical Jesus into a citizen of the twenty-first century. Here we strive to see him through the eyes of Mark. It remains a first-century perspective. Our concern is to under-stand the exorcism stories as signs of God's care for humankind and as promises of God's ultimate and total vic-tory over evil. In Jesus' view, they demonstrated that indeed "the kingdom of God is among you" (see Luke 17:21).

MESSIAH

The Lion of the tribe of Judah, the root of David, has conquered...then I saw a Lamb standing as though it had been slain. (Revelation 5:5–6)

"The beginning of the good news of Jesus Christ, the Son of God" (Mark 1:1). This superscription includes two of Mark's significant christological titles: Christ (Messiah) and

Son of God. We look, first, to the title *Messiah*. It is quite unlikely that Jesus himself ever claimed to be the Messiah. It is very likely, on the other hand, that some of his followers thought him to be the Messiah. It is also very likely that Jesus' opponents may have understood him or his followers to claim that he was the Messiah. After the resurrection, of course, Jesus was, by his followers, regularly called the Messiah— Jesus Christ (Messiah).

"He asked them, 'But who do you say that I am?' Peter answered him, 'You are the Messiah.'" In the evangelist's eyes, the unique significance of Peter's confession rests upon the fact that, for the first time, the disciples told Jesus who, in their estimation, he was. Jesus took the initiative and questioned the disciples about the opinion of "people" ("those outside," 4:11) and learned that they did not regard him as a messianic figure but, at most, as a traditional forerunner of the Messiah (8:27–28). Peter, however, had at last begun to see: "You are the Messiah." The sequel will show that his understanding of Jesus' messiahship was quite wide of the mark. This will be further discussed below.

SON OF DAVID

For Mark, the story of 10:46–52 sounds a new departure in the self-revelation of Jesus. He found himself acclaimed, repeatedly, as "Son of David." Far from imposing silence, he summoned the blind man to him and openly restored his sight. "Son of David" is a manifestly messianic title: Jesus is the messianic king, heir of the promise to David (2 Samuel

7:12–6; 1 Chronicles 17:11–14; Psalm 89:29–38). Jesus showed implicit approval of the title. There was no need of secrecy. Emphasis on suffering ever since Caesarea Philippi (8:31) had ruled out a triumphalist dimension.

Later, while teaching in the temple, Jesus himself raised the Son of David question: "How can the scribes say that the Messiah is the Son of David?" (12:35). It might seem that the question was designed to contest the Davidic descent of the Messiah. Rather, it was meant as a criticism of the scribes' understanding of Davidic messiahship, and so of their refusal to acknowledge the true personality of Jesus. Psalm 110, the opening verse of which is quoted in 12:36, is a royal psalm, addressed to the king—"my lord" is the king. Sitting at the right hand of Yahweh signifies the king's adoption as God's son (his representative), the acknowledged status of the Davidic king (2 Samuel 7:14). The argument here depends on the then current acceptance of the psalm as a composition of David (it is, in fact, later). On this supposition, David presents an oracle of Yahweh addressed to one whom he entitles "my Lord." The solemn attestation of David is underlined by the formula, unique in the Synoptic Gospels, "[inspired] by the Holy Spirit." This adds weight to the further question in verse 37: "David himself calls him lord; so how can he be his son?" If the great David had addressed the Messiah as "Lord," then the Davidic sonship of the Messiah must be understood in a sense that will acknowledge his superiority to David. The upshot is that Son of David, while it is a traditional title, is not really an adequate title. It does not capture the character of Jesus' messiahship.

SON OF GOD

The New Testament church confessed Jesus as Son of God and, in doing so, attributed to Jesus a unique relationship to God. The question then is: was the title *Son of God* bestowed on Jesus during his lifetime? The title was used, in association with Messiah, by the high priest (14:61), but the passage between the high priest and Jesus (14:61–62) reflects the Christology of the evangelist. The heavenly voice, at baptism and transfiguration, declaring Jesus to be "my Son, the Beloved" (1:1; 9:7) is for the sake of the readers. The confession of the Roman centurion (15:39) at that moment in the Gospel is a firm christological statement. Ironically, the one text in which Jesus referred to himself absolutely as the Son ("about that day or hour no one knows, neither the angels in heaven, nor the Son, but only the Father," 13:32) implies his subordination to the Father.

Abba

We can be sure that Jesus was conscious of a special relationship to God. This follows from his practice of regularly addressing God as *Abba*. Admittedly, in the Gospels the Aramaic word occurs only once—in Mark 14:36. But the term stands behind the Greek *pater*, "the Father," "Father," or "My Father" in Matthew 11:25–26; 26:39, 42; Luke 10:21–22; 11:1; 22:42; 23:34, 46. Several times, too, Jesus is said to address "the Father" (presupposing an original *Abba*) in prayer (for example, Matthew 11:25–26; Mark 14:36; Luke 23:34; John 17).

Our evidence, then, points to the fact that Jesus prayed to God as Abba. Now *Abba* was, in Jesus' time, a familiar and familial designation of one's father. There is no evidence that, in Palestinian Judaism, *Abba* was used in address to God. Jesus' usage is distinctive and suggests his consciousness of a unique relationship. Because he really *knew* his God, he could dare to call him Abba. And because he wished his disciples really to get to know God, he also wanted them to address prayer to God in the same manner. This is already present in Luke's version of the Lord's Prayer: "When you pray, say: Father [that is, Abba]" (11:1–2). That early Christians prayed so we know from Galatians 4:6 and Romans 8:15. They had recognized in Jesus' use of the title evidence of his religious experience of deep intimacy with God. And they were thankfully conscious of the fact that they had been brought to look at God through his eyes. They, too, had been led to *know* God.

The Secret

It was firmly Mark's view (his so-called "messianic secret") that no human being could acknowledge in faith and truth that Jesus is the Son of God before the paradoxical revelation of his identity through his death on the cross. At Jesus' baptism and transfiguration, the voice of God the Father did proclaim Jesus' Sonship. The demons also, with preternatural insight, could perceive what neither people nor disciples discerned: the true nature of Jesus. The unclean spirits became guides to the reader! That they are bound to silence is a reminder that to know and to proclaim the truth, one must, like the Roman centurion, come to terms with the cross (15:39).

The celebrated designation "Messianic Secret" is a misnomer. The element of secrecy concerns not Jesus' messiahship but his identity as Son of God. It follows that the titles *Messiah*, *King*, and *Son of Man*, are not, in the evangelist's estimation, wholly adequate. Mark takes care to identify his own evaluative point of view with that of the protagonist of his story: Jesus. Consequently, there is only one correct way in which to view things: the way of Jesus, which is also Mark's own way. The evangelist took a step further and made certain that both his assessment and that of Jesus were in accord with the point of view of God. It follows that the perception of Jesus that is normative in Mark's story is God's perception. If this is so, then the title that God bestowed on Jesus is of paramount importance.

The heading of the Gospel—"The beginning of the good news of Jesus Christ, the Son of God" (1:1)—informs the reader of Mark's own understanding of Jesus' identity. In the baptismal scene the heavenly voice (the voice of God) declared of Jesus: "You are my Son, the Beloved" (1:11). As Jesus was about to embark on his public ministry, God solemnly affirmed both his status and his call. Similarly, at the transfiguration, God declared (this time for the benefit of the three disciples), "This is my Son, the Beloved; listen to him!" (9:7). Only at Jesus' baptism and transfiguration does God emerge as "actor" in the story. And not alone did God each time declare that Jesus was "Son," but the declaration served the purpose of confirmation. The baptism declaration confirmed the truth of the caption (1:1); the trans-figuration declaration confirmed the truth of Peter's confession of Jesus as the "Messiah" (8:29). Finally, at the climactic moment of Jesus' death, the title was Son of God: "Truly, this man was God's Son" (15:39). The Roman centurion was the first human being in Mark's story to penetrate the secret of Jesus' identity, because he was the first to come to terms with the cross.

SUMMARY

The object of Christian faith is a living person, Jesus of Nazareth. He lived in the first century AD. He died—but lives forever, glorified, in the Father's presence. We have access to our living Lord through faith. The historical Jesus is not the object of our faith. He ought to be an integral part of our Christology. Dialogue with the historical Jesus guards our theology from degenerating into ideology.

Jesus of Nazareth was a prophet with a burning desire for the renewal of his people as God's holy elect. His challenge and his invitation were to all. He proclaimed the kingdom—the rule of God. The God of Jesus is a God with supreme concern for people. His rule, his lordship, envisaged an ideal relationship between God and humankind. Jesus lived and died for the establishment of that rule. He ached for men and women to discover the love of God for humankind and give substance to the wonder of the discovery in loving concern for one another.

Jesus preached the kingdom: he preached that God is the ultimate meaning of this world. The rule of God does not signify something "spiritual," outside of this world; it is not "pie in the sky." Jesus was supremely concerned with our real world. He spoke so vaguely of the future that the first Christians could expect that the end would come in their day (see Mark 9:1; 13:20). When he preached the kingdom of God, he envisaged a revolution in the existing order. He made two fundamental demands: he asked for personal conversion and he postulated a restructuring of the human world. Conversion (*metanoia*) meant changing one's mode of thinking and acting to suit God's purpose for humankind. It would be a new manner of existing before God.

But conversion also meant a turning from the established order. Jesus made the point, so clearly grasped and effectively developed by Paul, that it is not the law that saves—not even the Law—but rather love. Jesus' outlook and conduct were marked by freedom. His understanding of freedom is again faithfully reflected by Paul: freedom to serve. Jesus did not make life easier. His disconcerting word was that love knows no limits. He proclaimed not law but good news. The Gospel is good news for one who can grasp its spirit and react positively to it. His good news embraced basic equality: all men and women, as children of the Father, are brothers and sisters. Good news so understood is a radical challenge to all social and ecclesiastical systems based on power.

The prophet Jesus was in the line, too, of the sages of Israel. As teacher, no less than as prophet, he sought disciples. He called, and his call was a powerful summons. Discipleship meant wholehearted commitment; it was no soft option. His principle was that religion was meant to enable men and women to attain authentic humanness; it was not meant to enslave them. He took a firm stand against legalism. In light of God's preferential option for the poor, he warned of the threat of riches. Jesus was no respecter of persons. His declaration "It is easier for a camel to go through the eye of a needle than for someone who is rich to enter the kingdom of God" (10:25) would not be welcome in certain quarters. The gist of his teaching is found in his startling assertion that the essence of authority is service. If this were grasped and lived, much else would fall together. Until it is grasped and lived, authority in the church will continue to forfeit respect.

Jesus was a worker of miracles. In the main his activity was in the area of healing and covered a range of afflictions. He cured illness only in response to faith. Surely his deepest healing was at another level. His practice of table fellowship with sinners must have touched hearts. Mark perceptively observed that his "healing" had overtones of "saving" (*sozein*). And his opening of the eyes of the blind was an opening to more than the light of our world. A distinctive mode of healing was evidenced in his exorcisms. Here, Jesus struck at the heart of evil. He shared the apocalyptic worldview of his day. Good and evil were pitted in definitive struggle. His victories over evil were a presage of the undoubted ultimate victory of good. They were, already, earnest of the in-breaking of the rule of God—the kingdom.

CHAPTER 5

SUFFERING CHRIST

Mark's Christian community consisted of followers of Jesus who believed he was Christ and Son of God. Yet they had much to learn. The evangelist set out to declare who Jesus is, to spell out the nature of his messiahship. It is easy enough, he realizes, to declare, even with conviction: You are the Messiah. What matters is how one understands that confession. It does not ask too much of one to be a willing disciple of a risen Lord. We, all of us, find triumph and glory congenial. Mark takes an uncompromising stand. Jesus, is, of course, the Messiah and Son of God; he is the one who will, without fail, come to gather his elect. But he is also the suffering Son of Man, who walked a lone path to his death, who died, as it seemed to him, abandoned even by God. Mark stresses that only one who has come to terms with the cross can understand the resurrection of the Lord. Jesus was glorified because he had accepted the *kenosis,* the self-abasement, of his life and death. That is why Jesus was, for the first time, formally acknowledged by a human as Son of God as he hung lifeless on the tree (15:39).

Jesus is Messiah, of that Mark was sure, but he is a disconcerting Messiah. The question stands, writ large: "Who, then, is this?" That Jesus would have permitted himself to be taken by his enemies, to be maltreated and mocked by them and put to death, is something that the contemporaries of Jesus and the readers of Mark could hardly comprehend. Yet if one has not come to terms with this "scandal," one has not grasped the originality of Jesus, in particular, the Jesus portrayed by Mark. Jesus did not come as judge with sentence and punishment for those who would not accept the gift of forgiveness and salvation he offered to them. He had come as the one who would let himself be crushed by the evil intent of those who resisted him and would be rid of him.

At first sight, a suffering Son of Man, painfully vulnerable, and a Son of Man radiant in divine glory seem contradictory. In actual terms of the Jesus story, there is no contradiction. In Luke, the message was spelled out for the Emmaus disciples: "Was it not necessary that the Messiah should suffer these things and then enter into his glory?" (Luke 24:26). For Jesus, glory followed on suffering. It is the insight of the author of the book of Revelation: the Victim is the Victor. Glory beyond suffering is a concrete expression of the truth that *exousia* ("power," "authority") is most authentically present in *diakonia* ("service"). This is borne out by the two "earthly" Son of Man sayings: the Son of Man with authority to forgive sin, and the Son of Man, Lord of the Sabbath. Here is where, with urgency, the Son of Man is to be sought and found. Jesus, friend of sinners, mirrors a God of forgiveness. Jesus put people before observance. It was precisely because of his commitment to people, precisely because he was perceived as friend of sinners, that Jesus suffered the torture of the cross. It was precisely because of his commitment that God exalted him. When *exousia* is not *diakonia*, when forgiveness is not prodigal, the Son of Man is not being represented. The suffering Son of Man, rejected friend of sinners, must be embraced and confessed before any who claim to be his disciples can proclaim the Son of Man of glory. Mark is wholly consistent.

In the long run, what is incomprehensible is the rejection and death of the promised Messiah who would establish the rule of God, of the Son of God who would reveal the Father. The originality of Jesus flows from the contrast between his heavenly authority and power and the humiliation of his crucifixion. Mark's "messianic secret" is designed to reconcile two theological affirmations: Jesus, from the first, was indeed Messiah and yet had to receive from the Father, through the abasement of the cross, his title of Messiah. The meaning of his life is that as Son of God, sent by the Father, he had come to deliver men and women from all their enemies, from foes within and foes without. He came to forgive sins, not to condemn sinners. He came, but not to impose. When it came to the test, rather than force the human heart, he humbled himself and permitted himself to be taken and shamed and put to death.

COME TO SERVE

The prophet Jesus was on a mission. Jesus' mission was firmly political—by the very fact that it was conventionally apolitical. He did not side with any party. Inevitably, his "preferential option for the poor" brought him into conflict with the establishment of church and state. If Jesus' preaching of "good news to the poor" displayed a preference for the needy and the outcast, it was not an exclusive option. Rather, for him "poor" embraced the whole of humanity; those most in need were those who did not know their need. Jesus did not avoid his opponents; he dialogued with them. It is striking that so many of his extant parables are addressed to his opponents. True, he is critical of them and their tragic misunderstanding of God. But his criticism is motivated by his concern for them. It would not have been love to write them out of his life.

A Caring God

The message of Jesus, in word and deed, was *diakonia*, service. He came as the caring physician (see Mark 2:17), the friend of the outcast. His warm concern for the "poor," the little ones, brought him into conflict with those whose understanding of God was so different from his. Because he would not brand anyone an outcast, because he put ethics in place of ritual preoccupation, because he set people above observance, he was classed as a breaker of the law, as one who did not do the will of God. He remained faithful to the God he knew and he responded to the will of his loving Abba—though that faithfulness brought him to the cross. His death set humanity free because his life was laid down in defense of the value and dignity of the human person. In his life, sealed by the integrity of his death, Jesus gave expression to God's respect for humankind.

For this Jesus had been sent: to display the limitless love of the Father for humanity. He manifested that Father's love through his own loving concern for and service of all. Nothing could turn him from that way of love. He would lay down his life in the task, even when it meant that his life was crushed from him by those who could not or would not understand his service of love. But the Father understood that in this unswerving faithfulness to love lay the destruction of evil. This, too, is what Jesus meant when he spoke in the supper room of "my body which is given for you." Or when, in the Gospel of John, he spoke of that love than which none is greater, "that a man lay down his life for his friends" (John 12:13).

Obedient to the Will of God

The Son knew the Father and came to do his will. His life was not laid down in answer to divine need. It was laid down in answer to divine love. Father and Son were prepared to go to any length to save humans from themselves. The truth is that Jesus will save humankind though it cost him his life. And it did. And there, I believe, we find the ultimate meaning of the cry: "My God, my God, why have you forsaken me?" (Mark 15:4). Jesus is letting God be God. For it is in and through that emptiness—that openness—of the Son that the Father has given us everything, that he has made us his daughters and his sons.

Jesus began his mission with optimism. He did not start off with a grim vision of violent death at the end of the road. But as his mission progressed, he had to come to terms with the reaction and opposition that forced him to reckon with, first, the possibility and, then, the probability, of violent death. It is likely that the temptation stories, put at the start of the ministry by Matthew and Luke, really concern decisions made at a later stage. Gethsemane and the anguished cry from the cross witness to the agony of decision and the depressing prospect of failure.

THEOLOGY OF THE CROSS

Mark stands side by side with Paul as a stalwart proclaimer of a *theologia crucis*—a theology of the cross. And, congenial to modern Christology, the Markan Jesus is the most human of any. Jesus is Son of God, that is, God-appointed leader of the new covenant people; he is "son of man"—*this man*—the human one who came to serve, the one faithful unto death. One who has come to terms with the cross (the meaning of his death) can know him and can confess him—like the Roman centurion (15:39). His disciples did not understand him before Calvary. The Christian of the first century and of today is being challenged to come to terms with the love of God manifest in the cross of Jesus.

For Jesus, as for all of us, life was a pilgrimage—at more than one level. What Luke had to say of the twelve-year-old is perceptively true: "And Jesus increased in wisdom and in stature and in favor with God and man" (Luke 2:52). His journey was not only from Nazareth to the Jordan, from Galilee to Jerusalem. It was, above all, a journey of faith. Jesus, who knew the Father as no other did, still had to learn what it was the Father asked of him at the end of all. He found himself face to face with the stark reality of the cross: "...not what I will, but what you will." While fully aware that, in everything he did and said, he revealed the true God, he was to find that his last word was to be the revelation of what Paul would call the "foolishness" of God. The man himself was the revelation; his life and death the medium of his message.

The Pilgrimage

The pilgrimage of Jesus—*the* representative of our God—from a ministry of uninhibited love to death on a human-provided cross, is the great and ultimate human pilgrimage. No banners there, no colorful procession—despite an ephemeral welcome (Mark 11:1–10). Just disillusionment, shared by followers: "Jesus was walking ahead of them; and they were amazed, and those who followed were afraid" (10:32). They had caught the smell of disaster; the whiff was clear enough. Popular enthusiasm had waned: Jesus was no messianic warrior but a pacifist for the cause of God. Yet he had explicitly challenged the religious establishment by his criticism of Temple worship and of observance of the Torah. He was a heretic. He had implicitly challenged the Roman Empire. He was a rebel. It did not matter that his challenge was totally peaceful and wholly marked by love. He was walking the most precarious walk of all: the walk of one who holds for love in face of those who acknowledge only power, whether naked or subtly disguised. That awesome, and awful, journey to the cross is comfort to all who have seen in Jesus of Nazareth the image of the invisible God. It is the consola-

tion of all who have found in him the ultimate assurance that
God is on *our* side.

Unwavering Trust in God

Jesus had "set his face to go to Jerusalem" (Luke 9:51).
Mark's Gethsemane scene (14:32–42) shows that Jesus did
not fully understand God's way, that he did not want to die.
His Gethsemane decision was to trust God despite the darkness of his situation. He entrusted to God his own experience
of failure: his endeavor to renew Israel was being brutally
thwarted. His people had rejected him as they had, formerly,
rejected his Father. His cry of God-forsakenness on the cross
("My God, my God, why have you forsaken me?") speaks the
bitterness of his sense of failure. Contempt surrounded the
death of Jesus. Archaeology has shown that Golgotha, a dis-
used quarry, was a rubbish-dump. We have sanitized the Way
of the Cross and the cross itself. The reality was sordid. And
here we should remind ourselves that, as Christians, we know
about God through the humanity of Jesus. We need to
accommodate ourselves to the idea of a supreme being who
can fully reveal himself in this manner.

Jesus had not set out from Galilee to embrace the cross.
Throughout his ministry he had preached the rule of God—
God as salvation for humankind. His last, involuntary, sermon
was the most eloquent of all. The close of his earthly pilgrimage was to be his unequivocal proclamation of true divinity
and true humanity. For the cross is God's revelation of himself. It is there that he defines himself over against all human
caricatures of him. God, in the cross, is a radical challenge to

our *hubris*, our pride. There he is seen to be the *Deus human-issimus*—the God wholly bent on the salvation of humankind. No wonder that Paul can ask, in awe: "Since God did not withhold from us the most precious of all gifts, even the life of his own Son to give life to us all, can we not be certain that he would not possibly refuse us whatever else we may need?" (Romans 8:32).

WHO DO YOU SAY THAT I AM?

In the neighborhood of Caesarea Philippi, on the slopes of Mount Hermon (8:27), Jesus and his disciples are "on the way," ultimately the way to Jerusalem, the way of the cross. "He asked them, 'But who do you say that I am?'" (verse 29). In the evangelist's eyes the unique significance of Peter's confession rests on the fact that here, for the first time, the disciples told Jesus who, in their estimation, he was. Jesus took the initiative and put a direct question. Peter had at last begun to see: "You are the Messiah." The sequel will show that his understanding of Jesus' messiahship was wide of the mark.

Mark looked beyond Peter and the disciples to the community of his concern and bade his Christians take care that they really understood who their Christ is. There had been a studied preparation of the reader. From the start Mark had shown Jesus acting in an extraordinary manner that called forth the astonishment of the witnesses and led to a series of questions about him (1:27; 2:7; 6:20). Jesus himself heightened the effect (2:10, 28). Who is this Son of Man? Who is the Physician (3:16–17)? Who is this Bridegroom (2:19)? The themes of the amazement of the crowd and the incomprehension of the disciples stand as a question mark over the first eight chapters of the Gospel. And now, for the Christians who read Mark's Gospel, the confession "You are the Messiah" is their profession of faith. The warning is: that confession might be inadequate (8:32–33).

The central importance of Peter's confession in Mark's editorial structure is indicated by the brusque change of tone and of orientation after Peter has acknowledged the messiahship of Jesus. In the actual structure of the Gospel, the prediction of the passion (8:31–32a) is Jesus' response to the confession of Peter. The following section of the Gospel (8:31—11:10) is dominated by the prophecies of the passion (8:31; 9:31; 10:33–34), each of which is placed in a different geographical locale: Caesarea Philippi (8:27), Galilee (9:30), and on the way to Jerusalem (10:32). The heated protestation of Peter in 8:32 shows clearly that this is a new and unexpected teaching. "He said all this quite openly"—this is indeed a turning point in the self-revelation of Jesus, for until now he had said nothing explicitly about his messiahship. If he still charges his disciples not to reveal his messianic identity (verse 30)—because their understanding of him is still so imperfect—he now speaks to them quite plainly of his destiny of suffering and death. For, in Mark's intention, 8:31 becomes the starting point of the way of Jesus that ends in Jerusalem with the women at the tomb.

This passage, in truth, is less concerned with the historical situation of the mission of Jesus than with the historical situation of the church for which Mark is writing. The reply to

Jesus' first question refers to opinions available in the Palestinian situation of the ministry (verse 28). But, in the reply to the second question, the title *Messiah* (Christ) has Christian overtones, and the prediction of the passion is cast in language of the early church (verses 29 and 31). Peter's reaction and the sharp correction of it (verses 32–33) have much to do with an understanding of Christology. At the narrative level, Jesus and Peter engage in dialogue. At a deeper level, "Jesus" is the Lord addressing his church and "Peter" represents fallible believers who confess correctly but then interpret their confession mistakenly. Similarly, the "crowd" (verse 34) is the people of God for whom the general teaching (8:34—9:1) is meant. Thus, a story about Jesus and his disciples has a further purpose in terms of the risen Lord and his church.

Here, more obviously than elsewhere, Mark is writing for his community. Here, above all, he is concerned with Christology. The confession of Peter is the facile confession of too many of Mark's contemporaries: "You are the Messiah." Everything depends on what they mean by that profession and its influence on their lives. They cannot have a risen Lord without a suffering Messiah. They cannot be his disciples without walking his road of suffering. Mark's admonition here is quite like that of Paul in Romans 8:15–17.

The specific details of place (verse 27) and the designation of Peter as Satan (verse 33) show that an historical nucleus lies within 8:27–33. But the end product is Markan. On the basis of traditional data, the evangelist has carefully composed the whole central part, the hinge of his Gospel.

And in it he has shown that the messianic story is no uninterrupted success story: it is a story of suffering, rejection, failure. This fact must influence and color all we say about life and salvation. Jesus immediately runs into opposition: "Peter...began to rebuke him." Quite obviously, Peter has spoken for all of us. Jesus confirms this: "You are setting your mind...on human things"—the natural reaction of those who shrink from a way of suffering. Have we, at bottom, any different idea of salvation from that of Peter? Can we really conceive of salvation other than in categories of victory? We experience the saying of Jesus again and again as contradiction; we cannot reconcile ourselves to it. Jesus' rebuke did not change Peter; he will still deny the suffering Messiah. The other disciples will sleep and will abandon him. And the church, which began with the Twelve who failed to understand, will time and again like them, fail to understand.

What is the meaning of the word that follows the prediction of suffering and death: "...and after three days rise again"? These words are not meant to allay our fears, not meant to soften the stark reality of suffering and death. That word of victory of the Son of Man over death is promise of victory for the oppressed, the vanquished, the silent in death—the forgotten. It is a word of warning against our human way of exalting the victorious and triumphant. Through the suffering Messiah, victory is won by the vanquished; through the dead Messiah, life is regained by the dead. He and his way are the sole guarantee of our victory and of our life.

Prediction

The first of the predictions of the passion (8:31–33) is, in some way, the title of the second part of the Gospel, which begins at this point and will reach a climax on Calvary (15:39). "Then he began to teach"—these words suggest a new orientation in the teaching of Jesus. "He said all this quite openly" (8:32) might be rendered "And openly he proclaimed the word." This was the turning point in the self-revelation of Jesus. If he still charged his disciples not to reveal his messianic identity (verse 30), he now spoke to them quite openly of his messianic destiny of suffering and death. This emphatic affirmation that Jesus spoke openly *(parresia;* see John 7:26; 10:24) of his passion shows the unusual character of the fact. Even when he had spoken "privately" with his disciples he had never spoken so clearly. Here it is impossible to miss the meaning of his words, and Peter's reaction (verse 32b) shows that he had at once understood what Jesus had said, even though the divine necessity for the suffering escaped him altogether.

"And Peter took him aside": we can picture him, in his earnestness, taking hold of Jesus and "rebuking" him. He seems, for the moment, to have forgotten who was Master and who disciple. The notion of a suffering Messiah was quite foreign to Peter. His confession, "You are the Messiah," turns out to have been a classic instance of "verbal orthodoxy." The formula is correct; the understanding of it is quite mistaken. He realized, too, that his own situation would be affected; disciple of a suffering Messiah was not a role he relished. The phrase "and he looked at his disciples" is proper to Mark: the rebuke is addressed to them as well.

"Get behind me, Satan!" (*hypage opiso mou, Satana*)—the words recall Matthew 4:10, "Begone, Satan!" (*hypage, Satana*). This would suggest that Mark knew a form of the Matthew/Luke temptation story. The temptation in the wilderness (Matthew 4:1–11; Luke 4:1–13) aimed at getting Jesus himself to conform to a popularly envisaged messianic role, to become a political messiah. It was an attempt to undermine his full acceptance of the will of God for him, and here Peter was playing Satan's role. Peter's acknowledgment of Jesus as Messiah had, in principle, set him apart from "people" (verse 27), but now he found himself rebuked for judging in an all too human manner. Peter, and all like him who set their minds "on human things," stand opposed to God's purpose and align themselves with Satan.

Gethsemane

On the way to the Mount of Olives, Jesus spoke forebodingly of the fate of his disciples. He quoted Zechariah 13:7 to the effect that since Jesus the caring shepherd will be struck down, his defenseless sheep will be scattered. He then promised, in a reversal of the scattering, that after his resurrection he will again be their shepherd in Galilee; the flock will be reconstituted (see 16:7). Peter, who had earlier challenged Jesus (8:27–34), now again challenges him (14:29). Mark, like the other evangelists, has Jesus predicting Peter's threefold denial. Peter vehemently rebutted the warning and the others echoed his avowal of readiness to die with Jesus. The reader knows that the Twelve will fail abysmally, but Jesus will not abandon them. Mark is holding out hope to Christians who may fail.

We had not long to wait for the disciples to fail. All of them had heard his predictions of suffering and death; Peter, James, and John had heard the heavenly voice (9:7); James and John had confidently declared their readiness to share his cup (10:38–39). Now, at Gethsemane, he took the three to be with him in his hour of need—they do not perform as disciples. Jesus himself went apart to pray; he realized that he was on his own. Mark's Gethsemane scene shows that Jesus did not fully understand God's way and that he did not want to die. While we can plausibly assert that Abba was Jesus' preferred address to his God, the word *abba* occurs only once in the Gospels—here in Mark 14:36. There is a fittingness to its appearance here: the familiar title seems to be wrested from Jesus at this awful moment. He prayed explicitly that the cup be taken from him. He did not contemplate suffering and a horrible death with stoical calm. He was appalled at the prospect. He knew fear. He was brave as he rose above his dread to embrace what his God asked. But he must know if the path that opened before him was indeed the way that God would have him walk. He found assurance in prayer: the utterance of his trustful "Abba" already included "thy will be done." His decision was to trust God despite the darkness of his situation. His prayer did not go unanswered, although the answer was paradoxical. As the letter to the Hebrews puts it, "he was heard because of his reverent submission" (5:7). The obedient Son cried out to the Father and put himself wholly in the hands of the Father.

If Jesus said of the disciples, "the spirit indeed is willing, but the flesh is weak," that statement is not irrelevant to his own situation. Jesus himself had experienced human vulnerability: distress, agitation, and grief even to the point of death, to the point of asking the Father that the hour might pass him by and the cup be taken away. "Hour" and "cup" indicate the historical moment and the imminent prospect of appalling death. But this, too, was the eschatological hour of the final struggle, the great trial (*peirasmos*) before the triumph of God's kingdom. "The Son of Man is given over to the hands of sinners" (14:4). In the Old Testament, God gives over the wicked to punishment; here, in contrast, a just man is "given over" by God. At the end Jesus invited his disciples: "Get up, let us be going." Jesus still includes his disciples even though they had failed him.

It is important that Mark has so closely woven the theme of the disciples' misunderstanding with that of Jesus' testing. It is his most dramatic answer to any objection to a suffering Messiah. Jesus himself had been brought to the brink of rejecting it. The evangelist leaves no doubt that suffering messiahship is not easily accepted; he knows, as fully as Paul, that the cross is foolishness and scandal. The three disciples did not understand. The reader is duly warned. One must watch and pray. Good intentions are not enough. Discipleship is a way of life. And the course of that way has been plotted by Jesus: "Get up, let us be going…"

THE PASSION

Mark has firmly presented the passion of Jesus as proclamation of his kingship and the crucifixion as an enthronement. The theme appears at once in Pilate's question, "Are you the King of the Jews?" (15:2). Jesus did not reject the title out of hand but he did imply ("You have said so") that he understood it differently. Pilate repeatedly calls him King of the Jews (verses 9 and 12). Indeed, in verse 12 he is "the man whom you (the chief priests) call the King of the Jews." The soldiers paid homage to "the King of the Jews" (verses 16–19), and the official charge against Jesus read: "The King of the Jews" (verse 26). Priests and scribes mocked him as "the Messiah, the King of Israel" (verse 32). If, for Mark, this is a narrative of the enthronement of Christ as king, it is such in light of Jesus' profession of 14:62, which sealed his fate (verses 63–64). Jesus' royal status is wholly paradoxical. Jesus' regal authority could never resemble the authority of earthly kings (see 10:42–45).

And They Crucified Him

There is a strange poignancy about the death of Jesus, a tragic quality that is caught superbly by Mark. Jesus' death was brought about by human connivance. Jesus was at once a religious and a political hazard. His preaching of good news to the poor was a threat to the establishment, a threat to church and state. That voice had to be silenced. Together they condemned him to death. As he moved toward the cross, Jesus was left more and more alone: betrayed by one disciple, denied by another, abandoned by all. Even his fellow sufferers disowned him. Most terrible of all, he suffered the absence of God: "My God, my God, why have you forsaken me?" (15:34). He now knows what it costs to give his life as a ransom for all (10:45).

The grim drama was being played out. Crucified at the third hour (9:00 A.M.), Jesus had spent three hours in agony. Now, at the sixth hour (noon), the hour of darkness and of momentary demonic triumph, broke in —"your hour, and the power of darkness" (Luke 2:53; see Amos 8:9–10). Jesus had begun his mission in an encounter with Satan (Mark 1:12–13) and carried on the war in his exorcisms. Now, helpless on the cross, he seemed to be crushed by these very powers. The close of that time of darkness (symbolic theological darkness), the ninth hour (3 pm), marked the hour of fulfillment. Paradoxically, it seemed to sound the nadir of Jesus' defeat. This is brought out by the twofold reference to a "loud cry"—*phone megale* in Greek. Mark uses this expression four times: twice to describe the loud cry of the demoniac (1:26 and 5:7) and twice referring to the reaction of Jesus himself to the intolerable pressure of evil (15:34, 37). He suffered the absence of God. His cry of dereliction was one of total desolation: "My God, my God, why have you forsaken me?" His words are the opening of Psalm 22, a lament. A lament is the cry of a suffering righteous person addressed to the One who can bring an end to suffering. Mark has Jesus die in total isolation, without any relieving feature at all. It would have seemed that, up to this point, Jesus' isolation could go no further: deserted by his disciples, taunted by his enemies, derided by those who hanged with him, suffocating in the darkness of evil. But the worst was now. His suffering was radically lonely. But his God was *my* God (verse 34). Even in this, as at Gethsemane, it was "not what I want, but what you want." Here, even more than earlier, the sheer humanness of Jesus was manifest. And his experience was a thoroughly human one. It underlines the difference between feeling and reality. The feeling: one of God-forsakenness. The reality: never were Father and Son more at one. It is akin to the experience of Job, who also suffered the absence of God, or of later mystics suffering the "dark night of the soul." God had never withdrawn; the feeling was that he had.

The bystanders thought that Jesus had called on Elijah (verse 35), who was popularly believed to come to the aid of the just in tribulation. Misunderstanding hounded Jesus to the end. "Sour wine" is the Roman soldiers' *posca*—a cheap red wine. The gesture was kindly meant (verse 36), but Mark, likely with Psalm 69:21 in mind ("They gave me gall for my food, and for my thirst they gave me vinegar to drink"), thinks of it as an addition the Jesus' misery. Once again, the "loud cry" is significant: it depicts his consciousness of his struggle with evil. All the more so because verse 37 describes a sudden, violent death; "breathed his last" is not strong enough to carry Mark's meaning. Jesus died abandoned, seemingly crushed by the forces of evil. This is perfectly in keeping with Mark's *theologia crucis*. Forthwith, he will be able to point to the victory of Jesus.

At the end of the passage, verses 27–39, Mark focuses on the theme of Jesus as "the Son of God." An emphatically positive response to Jesus' death contrasts with the mocking challenges hurled at the dying Jesus (15:29–32), when the Roman centurion in charge declares in awe: "Truly, this man was God's Son!" (verse 39). Note that the temple curtain had just been rent from top to bottom (verse 38): the temple had lost its significance (see 11:12–25; 13:2; 14:58) as center of the cult through which God had mediated forgiveness of sin and salvation. The temple curtain "was torn"—by God! Jesus, who had suffered the pangs of God-forsakenness, was now vindicated. Salvation is henceforth mediated through the shedding of the blood of the Son of God. As Jesus had proclaimed to his disciples, "the Son of Man came not to be served but to serve, and to give his life as a ransom for many [all]" (10:45) through his blood "which is poured out for many [all]" (14:24). The temple is gone. God's Son is now the locus of salvation. While the chief priests had demanded that "the Messiah, the King of Israel, come down from the cross now, so that we may see and believe" (verse 32), it was a Gentile who saw and believed. The Roman centurion's is a profession of Christian faith. It confirms Mark's theological position. The revelation of God's Son took place on the cross.

TO THE END

"Jesus…having loved his own who were in the world, he loved them to the end" (John 13:1). "To the end" (*eis telos*) means more than steadfastness to the last. The phrase can be adequately rendered in some such fashion: he showed them how utterly he loved them. Jesus would show his "greater love" (John 15:13) by dying for the principles he steadfastly believed in, principles he so earnestly wanted his disciples to embrace. He knew that his death would awaken them to the seriousness of his demands and would inspire them to be faithful to his ideal. They, in turn, would display to the world the true visage of the Father. It was the Father who inspired Jesus himself.

Jesus laid down his life in loving response to the Father's love. The Father did not demand the death of Jesus; the Father did not seek the death of Jesus. The Father gave his Son for humankind—but gave him *eis telos*. He would show human beings that his love for them was in deadly earnest. The Father did not bring about the death of his Son; Jesus died at the hands of his religious and political enemies. But the Father did not shrink from having him "delivered up" to his enemies. Only so does the death of the Son fall within "the definite plan and foreknowledge of God" (Acts 2:23). And, in filial acceptance of God's saving purpose, and only so, did Jesus accept death. He was obedient unto death, with an obedience that was a loving "Yes" to a purpose of sheerest love. "God so loved the world…" There is no gainsaying that word. It is the only explanation of the death of Jesus that is consonant with the character of our God.

God-with-Us

In 16:1–8, Mark relates that the three women who had witnessed the burial of Jesus (15:40), intending to anoint his body, bought spices when the Sabbath had ended. Their purpose is in step with the hasty burial (15:46). The large stone that sheltered the body would have presented a problem. To their surprise, they found that the stone "had already been rolled back." This is the divine passive: God had acted.

The "young man" dressed in white is an angel. They had come seeking Jesus; they had seen where his body had been laid. Again they look upon the spot, but he is no longer there. The "young man" plays the role of *angelus interpres,* of interpreting angel, a feature of apocalyptic. They were faced with the riddle of an empty tomb. He explains why the tomb is empty: "He has been raised." Mark has to intimate that death was not the end. But he takes care to refer to resurrection as briefly as possible. He will not divert his emphasis from the Roman centurion's profession of faith (15:39).

Resurrection

Jesus had died with the cry on his lips: "My God, my God, why have you forsaken me?" The sequel was to show that God had never abandoned Jesus. We have the assurance that he will never abandon us. If the life of Jesus shows the meaning of his death, the life and death of Jesus show the meaning of his resurrection. As Jesus' lifestyle, his praxis of the rule of God, had prepared him for his death, his being raised from death was the vindication of all he stood for. This involves more than the authentication of his message. Resurrection, for one thing, underlines the reality of Jesus' Abba-consciousness, his communion with God, which death could not disrupt. The resurrection of Jesus demonstrates that God is indeed the God of humankind who holds out, to all of us, the promise of life beyond death. In other words, the resurrection of Jesus is not only something that happened to him—it reaches to us. And not only as it concerns our future life. Already, as risen Lord, Jesus himself is present to us in our striving to give substance to the rule of God. He is Emmanuel, God-with-us (Matthew 1:23; see 28:29).

"God was in Christ, reconciling the world to himself" (2 Corinthians 5:19). As Christians, we see our God in Jesus of Nazareth. If we are to let God be God, we must let Jesus be Jesus. Christology—the theological understanding of Jesus Christ—cannot be unveiling of mystery. We must let the mystery abide. And the mystery is the person Jesus of Nazareth. To diminish the human reality is to screen from sight the God who would shine through him. Christology has tended to do just that. We need to acknowledge a vulnerable Jesus if we are to meet our vulnerable God. The mystery of Jesus is that in him God communicates himself in a full and unrestricted manner. Jesus' divinity is not, as sometimes presented, some kind of second substance in him. His divinity consists in the fact that, as the perfect counterpart of God, he is the manifestation and presence of God in our world. Any misperception that "Jesus is human, but…"—and such misperceptions are all too common—is effectively a refusal of the God who revealed himself in Jesus. When the human Jesus is not acknowledged, our understanding of God suffers and our Christianity suffers. This not to say that the full reality of Jesus may be adequately summed up under the rubric "human being"—there is something other, something much more. But his human wholeness must be acknowledged.

The career of Jesus did not end on the cross. The resurrection is God's endorsement of the definition of both God and humankind made on the cross. Just as the death of Jesus cannot be detached from the life lived before it, his resurrection cannot be detached from his career and death. Because he was raised from the dead, Jesus holds decisive significance for us. Because of the fact of his resurrection we know that meaningless death—and often meaningless life—has meaning. Jesus died with the cry on his lips: "My God, my God, why have you forsaken me?" The sequel was to show that God had not forsaken Jesus. We have the assurance that he will not abandon us. While we, unlike his immediate disciples, do not follow the steps of Jesus from Galilee to Jerusalem, we do join his human pilgrimage from birth to death. His word of promise is that we shall follow him beyond death to share his rest (see Hebrews 12:2). We shall know fully our Abba and become wholly his children.

TRIUMPH OF FAILURE

Mark was keenly aware of the paradox at the heart of Christianity, a paradox dramatically presented by the author of the book of Revelation: the Victim is the Victor. The story of Jesus as told in Mark's Gospel is a story of human failure: the failure of Israel, the failure of the disciples, the seeming failure of Jesus himself. Yet Jesus, the Son of God, won through to "resurrection life" by his openness to the ways of God. Faithfulness to God led him to acceptance of death on a cross, thereby becoming Messiah and Son of God. In his mission,

Jesus sought to draw others into a following of this way. Failure of the disciples reached its climax in their flight at the arrest of Jesus (14:50). It seemed that women disciples had redeemed the situation. They, albeit at a distance, witnessed the crucifixion (15:40), saw where the body had been laid (15:47), and later came to anoint it (16:1). Assured that Jesus had been raised from the dead (16:6), they were commanded to take the Easter message to the failed disciples (16:7). Mark has the last, unexpected word: "So they went out and fled from the tomb, for terror and amazement seized them; and they said nothing to any one, for they were afraid" (16:8). In the end, the women join the men disciples in failure, sharing both their fear and flight.

Ultimately, all humans fail. God alone succeeds. The Father had not abandoned the Son (15:34) but had raised Jesus from the dead (16:6). The failed disciples will encounter the risen Lord in Galilee (14:28; 16:7), not because they have succeeded, but solely because of the initiative of God. Fulfillment of the promise (14:28; 16:7) is not in the text of Mark's Gospel. It is in the Christian community that received the story.

The conclusion of Mark's Gospel is not a message of failure but a resounding affirmation of God's design to overcome all imaginable failure (16:1–8) in and through the action of God's beloved Son (1:1–13). The words addressed to the struggling disciples at the transfiguration are addressed to all who take up the call of the Gospel: "Listen to him" (9:7).[1]

CHAPTER 6

WALKING THE WAY

"Immediately he regained his sight and followed him on the way." (Mark 10:32)

We begin this study of "walking the way"—of discipleship—by looking to Jesus' own relationship with his immediate disciples. We should have in mind Mark's distinctive preoccupation with the disciples' misunderstanding of Jesus. The other evangelists make clear that his disciples did, even before Easter, grasp some of Jesus' teaching. Mark, however, indicates the demands of discipleship.

DISCIPLESHIP

Can we discern Jesus' own understanding of discipleship? At the close of a careful study, scripture scholar John Meier has shown what it meant to be a historical disciple of the historical Jesus:

(1) Jesus seized the initiative in deciding who would be his disciples. He confronted certain individuals with his imperious demand to follow him, a command that brooked no opposition or delay. (2) Hence, in using the term "following," Jesus intended not some pious metaphor but literal, physical following of his preaching tours around Galilee. Accordingly, those who accepted his command to follow had to leave behind home, family, and other comfortable ties. (3) On top of these hardships, Jesus warned his disciples that they might face other sufferings: hostility and even deadly opposition, including opposition from one's alienated family.[1]

The Call

Jesus began his mission by summoning disciples. The passage 1:16–20, with two parallel episodes, was shaped by Mark to bring out the nature of Jesus' call and the nature of Christian response—in short, to show what "following Jesus" means. We are shown that the sovereign call of Jesus evokes the response of those called, a free response, as we will learn in the episode of the man who could not bring himself to follow—the man "who had great possessions" (10:17–22). These fishermen leave all—nets, boat, and father—to follow Jesus without hesitation. The decisive factor is the person of Jesus himself. The episode is stylized, of course. Mark is not intent on describing a scene from the ministry of Jesus. Rather, he is concerned with the theological dimension of a typical call to discipleship. Behind his text, however, is the memory that Jesus called—the initiative was his—and that his immediate disciples, men and women (see 15:40–41), had indeed left all to accompany him on his itinerant mission. We must keep in mind that others had responded to Jesus without taking to the road with him—people like the sisters Martha and Mary of Bethany. There are different ways of true discipleship.

The passage 1:16–20 gives the call of the first four immediate followers of Jesus. The number was to grow. We do not know how many disciples there eventually were. It must have been sizable enough to accommodate the inner core of the Twelve. It had been assumed that all of the disciples were men, but this was to ignore significant evidence to the contrary. If, at the arrest of Jesus, "all of them deserted him and fled" (14:50), a little group of women remained. Mark says of them: "They used to follow him and provide for him while he was in Galilee, and there were many other women who had come up with him to Jerusalem" (verse 41). The women had "followed him" —*akolouthein* is a technical term for discipleship. And they "served" Jesus: they are authentic disciples (10:43–45). Although this is the only place in Mark where the discipleship of women is mentioned in explicit terms, we should not overlook that reference to "many other women." We must recognize that, throughout the Gospel, "disciple" is an inclusive term.

The Twelve

Historically, the Twelve, the inner circle within the group of disciples, had a symbolic role. In his proclamation of the kingdom of God, Jesus looked to the dynamic event of God coming in power to rule his people Israel in the end time. In line with the hope of post-exilic Judaism, he envisaged it as the regathering in the end time of all Israel, all twelve tribes. The Twelve symbolized that reconstituted Israel. In this context, the mission of the Twelve (6:7–13) should be viewed as a prophetic gesture: the regathering had begun. After an initial concern to restore the number twelve following on the defection of Judas (Acts 1:15–26), it was evidently understood that the Twelve belonged specifically in the historical mission of Jesus. Mark, it would seem, viewed the Twelve as exemplars of discipleship. We will regard them in this light.

The call of the Twelve (see 3:13–19) was a solemn moment. The bracket-phrase "he appointed twelve" underlines the immediate role of this inner group. In the first place, they are "to be with him"; they are to have a close personal relationship with Jesus—forming a new family, in short. And from now on the Twelve do remain constantly with him (until they fail him, spectacularly, 14:50). In the second place, the Twelve were commissioned to be sent out, to preach, and to have authority over demons. While the evangelist had the sending out of 6:7–13 in mind, his vocabulary shows that he looked beyond it. The Greek words *apostellein*, "to send out," and *keryssein*, "to preach," are terms used by the apostolic church to describe its mission. Mark was conscious of the post-resurrection missionary situation. The Twelve were to preach and to do; the word of God is proclaimed in word and action together.

Jesus had been rejected by the people of his hometown, Nazareth (6:1–6a). Now he turns his attention to the Twelve. He had chosen them "to be with him" and he had concentrated on instructing them. But he had also chosen them "to be sent out and to proclaim the message"; the time has come for them to take an active part in his mission. They are given authority over unclean spirits; up until now Jesus alone exercised this authority. The disciples now share in the mission of Jesus. But unlike Matthew and Luke (see Matthew 10:7; Luke 9:2), Mark carefully avoids stating that they proclaimed the kingdom. In his perspective, the disciples have not yet understood the true nature of the kingdom. Like John the Baptist (1:4), they preached "that all should repent" (verse 12).

The sending out of the disciples "two by two" (6:7) follows Jewish practice. In a summarizing passage (verses 12–13), Mark's reference to the preaching of repentance is deliberate. In his plan the preaching of the imminence of the kingdom is reserved to Jesus; the disciples, like the Baptist, prepare for Jesus' proclamation. If the disciples do now share in the mission of Jesus, it is only in association with Jesus that their mission can prosper. They will learn to their cost (see 9:14–29) that apart from him they can do nothing (John 15:5).

True Discipleship

Coming directly after the first prediction of the passion (8:31–33), 8:34—9:1 asserts unequivocally that the disciples of the Son of Man (verse 31) must necessarily walk in his path. Jesus had "called the crowd and his disciples" (verse 34): this challenge is addressed to all. The loyal disciple would not be preoccupied with personal interests but would follow in sustained faithfulness to Jesus. The way of discipleship is not easy and one may be tempted to shrink from what it entails. To seek thus to evade risk and save one's life—to have things one's way—would be to suffer the loss of one's true self. One prepared and willing to risk all for Jesus and for the good news is one who will achieve authentic selfhood. If human life on earth is so much more precious than anything else in creation, if no one can put a price on it, how much more precious the eternal life to be won by the faithful disciple. There is the challenge. A warning sounds for one who would draw back, ashamed of the Way, one who would seek to save one's life (see 4:14–19). Jesus, too, the warning rings, will be ashamed of such a one, will not acknowledge such a one, when he will reappear in glory at the end (verse 38). But "some standing here" will be witnesses of the vindication of the Son of Man ("after three days rise again," 8:31). Their witness sustains the faith of the Markan community. Mark was still certain that a Christian had to come to terms with the cross. Once this had been grasped, one had to spread the good news (see 13:10).

Mark assuredly looked beyond the mission of Jesus. Like the author of the book of Revelation, his concern was for the persecuted community of his day (see 13:9–13), although, in neither case, was it yet all-out persecution. He reminded those followers of a rejected and crucified Messiah that it should not surprise that they, too, were called on to suffer. The cross had turned the values of the world upside down—it is indeed a "stumbling block" and "foolishness" (see 1 Corinthians 1:23).

They must be steadfast in face of persecution. They must not be ashamed of Jesus' way of humiliation and suffering and death, if they do not want the glorious Son of Man to be ashamed of them at his coming (Mark 8:38).

Persecution

In the Farewell Discourse (chapter 13), Mark warns that persecution may well be the lot of Christian disciples. Noteworthy is the threefold repetition of "to deliver up" (verses 9b, 11a, and 12a): persecution and suffering are their lot, as for their master. They will be hauled before Jewish tribunals (verse 9a) and Gentile authorities (verse 9b). Paradoxically, these Christians, although in the guise of arraigned prisoners, will be bearing witness to the Name. Even more strangely—for God's ways are not the ways of humankind—persecution will be an occasion of a wider mission to the Gentiles (verse 10; see Acts 8:1–5). For that matter, one might say that Christian suffering is itself that proclamation: by suffering as Jesus suffered, they are making him present in their world. For Mark, it is wholly fitting that the suffering and death of Christians should open the way to the Gentiles. Already he had shown that the death of the precursor had coincided with the first sending of the Twelve on their mission (6:7–30). He will show that the death of Jesus tears away the veil of division between Jew and Gentile (15:38; see Ephesians 2:11–22). Moreover, by asserting that the Gospel must "first" be preached, Mark is asserting that the gathering in of the full number of the Gentiles (see Romans 11:35) is part of God's plan. In their trials, Christians are assured of help (verse 11). It is not said that the Spirit will speak up on behalf of the disciples. Rather, they are assured of the help of the Spirit; and the preparation of the defense is less the drafting of an apologia than a prayer. Here is a sign and promise of God's help in trouble.

Servant

In 9:35–37, Mark has made the point that the revelation of Jesus cannot be received by one who is not ready to enter into the spirit of discipleship and thereby become "last" and "servant": "Whoever wants to be first must be last of all and servant of all" (9:35). As it stands, the passage is a pronouncement story; the point of it lies in the sayings of 35b and 37, with the gesture of verse 36 (taking a little child) underlining the lesson. Jesus acknowledges that there is greatness in discipleship, the greatness of service. And this is so because the loving service of the least member of the community is service of Jesus and of the Father. At the start ("when he was in the house," verse 33), Mark had drawn the special attention of his readers to this teaching and to all that will be said until verse 50. Perhaps the reader of today is once again attuned to the unambiguous message of this word of Jesus: greatness in his church is found in *diakonia* ("service") and only there. This word was heard at the Second Vatican Council. Our first step is to have relearned it. It is high time for us to act accordingly. Sadly, it seems that the word is not heard where one might have expected it to be welcomed.

The point of the related narrative of 10:13–16 lies in the sayings. The disposition of a child—receptivity, a willingness to accept what is freely given—is necessary for all who would enter the kingdom. Children, better than anyone else, are suited for the kingdom, since the kingdom is a gift to be received with simplicity. Jesus himself, in a true sense, is the kingdom; that is why, in the episode, children have a right of access to him. The solemn "Amen" ("Truly I tell you") confirms the seriousness of the pronouncement of verse 15: "Truly I tell you, whoever does not receive the kingdom of God as a little child will never enter it." One must receive the kingdom as a child receives it, with trustful simplicity and without laying any claim to it. Here, the kingdom appears both as gift that people receive and as a sphere into which they enter: one must be willing to receive the kingdom as gift before one can enter into the blessings and responsibilities of it.

Faith

Jesus looked for faith: trust in a faithful and gracious God. Indeed, faith is, along with salvation, one of the major themes of the twin narratives of Jairus' daughter and the woman who suffered from a chronic hemorrhage (5:21–43). Jairus had faith that Jesus' touch would heal his daughter (verse 23), and the woman had faith that by touching Jesus' garments she would be healed (verse 28). The verb used in both passages is *sozo*, which means "to save" as well as "to heal" or "to make well." Jairus had begged for his daughter to be made well "and live." The verb here meaning "to live," *zao*, in a Christian context had assumed overtones of enjoying eternal life. In other words, "That she may be saved and have eternal life." In verse 34, Jesus reassured the woman, telling her, "your faith has made you well—has saved you." Mark had in mind more than bodily healing. Salvation stands in close relationship to faith. Jesus then enjoined Jairus, "Do not fear, only believe" (verse 36).

Faith comes to fulfillment in personal encounter with Jesus, in dialog with him. Jairus believed that Jesus had power to heal one on the point of death (verse 23). Jesus looked for a deeper faith: faith in him as one who could rise from the dead, a faith finding expression in the midst of unbelief (verses 35–36). The woman, too, had faith in the power of Jesus (verses 27–28). She, too, was asked to have a fuller faith in him; she met his gaze and came to kneel at his feet (verse 33). Through faith in Jesus, she and the girl were made well—saved. The Christian is asked to recognize that faith in Jesus can transform life and bring victory over death. This faith is not something vague or impersonal: one must kneel at his feet, not abjectly, but in the intensity of one's pleading (verse 22) or in humble thankfulness (verse 33). This Jesus will give to the believer that peace the world cannot give; he will assure that person of life beyond death (verse 34).

In 9:14–29, the healing of an epileptic boy, the motif of faith is firmly stressed. Jesus upbraided the faithless generation: all—scribes and Pharisees, the people, his very disciples—have been hardhearted and without understanding. And the boy's father had doubted the power of Jesus: "If you are able!" (verse 22). He was told that faith does not set limits to the power of God. His cry ("I believe, help my unbelief!") is the heart of the story. He acknowledged his lack of faith and looked to Jesus for help. At that moment he stood in sharp contrast to the Twelve, who displayed their lack of trust. He is typically one of the "little people" who believe. Jesus lifted up one who looked like a corpse, who was reckoned to be dead (verses 26–27). Now the disciples learned what rising from the dead meant: Christ's victory over the forces of evil. Now they recognized the power and authority of Jesus. Only through union with their Lord in prayer will they share that same power (verse 29). Bereft of his presence, stripped of communion with him, Christians are powerless and helpless.

Love of God

In a pronouncement story (12:28–34), Jesus gives his answer to the question, "Which commandment is the first of all?" It was a question the rabbis sought to answer. They looked for the Torah commandment that outweighed all the others, one that might be regarded as a basic principle on which the whole Law was grounded. We find something of this in Matthew's declaration: "On these two commandments hang all the law and the prophets" (Matthew 2:40). Because it is an honest question by one well disposed (Mark 12:32–34), Jesus answers directly. He begins by quoting the opening formula (Deuteronomy 6:4) of the *Shema,* the "creed" recited by every male Israelite morning and evening, and joins to it Leviticus 19:18, which enjoins love of neighbor. He had been asked to name the first commandment; he responds by naming two commandments. This is of major importance. It would seem that Jesus was the first to bring together these two commands of love of God and love of neighbor, because for Jesus the one flows directly, and necessarily, from the other. Love for neighbor arises out of love of God. He had taken and welded the two precepts into one.

In the Synoptic Gospels, only here and in Luke 11:42, which is derivative of Mark, is there word of humans' love of God, and it appears sparingly in the rest of the New Testament. Usually, the emphasis is on God's love for humankind. And this is as it should be. It is because God has first loved us that we love God (Romans 5:5, 8; 1 John 4:11). Indeed, love for one another is the test of the reality of our love of God (1 John 4:20–21). Jesus himself showed in his life and death the quality of this twofold love. His love for God motivated his total dedication to his mission; his love for humankind marked him as one who had come to serve the saving purpose of God, one who had laid down his life as a ransom for humanity (Mark 10:45).

The scribe's reply (12:32–33) is proper to Mark. He agrees fully with Jesus' answer and further specifies that the true love of God and the loving service of others are more important than elaborate cult. In insisting on love with the whole heart, he recognizes that love cannot be measured. Love is incompatible with a legalism that sets limits, that specifies what one should do and should avoid. Jesus' assurance (verse 34) that this scribe is not far from the kingdom of God is, in truth, an invitation. It is a challenging invitation to any who would walk the way.

Prayer

As an observant Jew, Jesus was a man of prayer. Mark, who understood this, mentions prayer of Jesus on three occasions: at Capernaum (1:35), after the multiplication of loaves (6:46), and in Gethsemane (14:35, 39). Early in his Gospel (Mark 1:21–24), the evangelist has sketched a sample day in the early Galilean mission, at Capernaum, a day of enthusiastic reception and of great promise. His disciples, caught up in the excitement, were chagrined when Jesus went missing (verse 37): "In the morning, while it was still very dark, he got up and went out to a deserted place, and there he prayed" (1:35). Typically, Mark has said so much in few words. Jesus had slept (he "got up"), had snatched a few hours of sleep. For his mission he needed deeper refreshment, a more potent source of energy, and he found it in prayer to his Abba.

It is to be expected that Jesus meant his disciples to pray. Mark took this so much for granted that he rarely alludes to prayer. After the cure of the epileptic boy (9:14–27), he depicts Jesus alone with his disciples "in a house" where they questioned him "privately" *(kat' idian)*. This esoteric message to the disciples is, in reality, addressed to the Christian community. "This kind can come out only through prayer" (verse 29): Jesus explained why the disciples had been unable to cope with the unclean spirit. Prayer was vitally necessary: the healer must rely wholly on the power of God. Some manuscripts add "and fasting." Its addition is understandable but wrongheaded. Fasting would add something of one's own effort, whereas the point being precisely made is total reliance on the Lord. The disciples had been on their own and helpless. We, as the disciples of our day, must learn that only through union with our Lord in prayer can we function. Bereft of his presence, stripped of communion with him, Christians are powerless and helpless.

Eucharist

A particularly solemn and essentially central form of prayer was soon established in Christian practice: the Lord's Supper. Mark introduces it in the setting of Jesus' Farewell Supper (14:12–25). He does present it as a Passover meal; in fact, the Last Supper was a solemn farewell meal, not a traditional Passover meal.

Mark has placed the announcement-of-betrayal passage in the setting of eucharistic table fellowship, between preparation for the Supper (14:12–16) and the Supper itself (verses 22–25). It is a chastening admonishment to the reader. Just as Paul challenges his readers, "Examine yourselves, and only then eat of the bread and drink of the cup" (1 Corinthians 11:28), so too the Christian must ask, "Is it I?"—do I betray the Lord Jesus?

The phrase "While they were eating" (verse 22) resumes the meal episode after the warning of betrayal (verses 17–21). Jesus "took bread," "blessed," "broke," and "gave"—traditional eucharistic language. "This is my body." In 1 Corinthians 11:22, Paul adds, "which is for you." But this is already firmly implied in Mark through the repeated references to Jesus' death since the beginning of the passion narrative and the explicit statement in the cup saying, "This is my blood of the covenant." Exodus 24:8 is certainly in mind: "See the blood of the covenant that the Lord has made with you." By the sprinkling of sacrificial blood the people of Israel shared in the blessings of the covenant given on Mount Sinai. Likewise this blood of the cup will be poured out "for many" (a Semitism meaning "all"): a new covenant is being forged and sealed whose blessings are offered to all. The death of Jesus founds the new community. The Last Supper helps us to understand the meaning of Jesus' death on Calvary.

The Last Supper narrative (verses 22–25) is based on the liturgical tradition of Mark's community. While less explicit than the Pauline tradition (1 Corinthians 11:23–26), it has the same meaning. In both, the eucharistic meal anticipates the eschatological banquet of the kingdom. And if Mark does not have Paul's "Do this in remembrance of me," the eucharistic liturgy of his church was the living fulfillment of that word.

THREATS TO DISCIPLESHIP

Riches

In his discipleship demand (8:34–38), Jesus had asked of aspiring disciples: "What will it profit you to gain the whole world and forfeit your life?" (verse 36). The allure of wealth is a threat to true discipleship. Jesus' teaching on the hazard of riches (10:23–27) and on the reward of renunciation (verses 28–31) was prompted by the incident of verses 17–22. This is the saddest story in the Gospel, this story of the refusal of one whom Jesus loved to answer his call. Entry into the kingdom is the issue as Jesus was asked what one must do to inherit eternal life. He began to answer the question by pointing to the duties toward one's neighbor prescribed by the decalogue, but he knew that observance of law was not the whole answer. He was drawn to the man and invited him to become his disciple. This aspiring disciple had to learn that discipleship is costly: he, a wealthy man, was asked to surrender the former basis of his security and find his security in Jesus' word. He failed to see that following Jesus was the true treasure, the one pearl of great price (Matthew 13:44, 46), beyond all his possessions. He could not face the stern challenge of loving in deed and in truth by opening his heart to his brother or sister in need (see 1 John 3:17–18). He was not receptive.

The rich man's sad departure (Mark 10:22) was dramatic evidence that riches could come between a person and the following of Jesus; the words of Jesus (verses 23–27) drove the message home. Jesus began by stressing the difficulty, for the wealthy, of access to the kingdom (verse 23) and passed quickly to the difficulty of entering the kingdom at all (verse 24). A vivid example of the impossible—"It is easier for a camel to go through the eye of a needle than for someone who is rich to enter the kingdom of God" (verse 25), a contrast of the largest beast known in Palestine with the smallest domestic aperture—applied as it is to the rich, would come more logically before verse 24. The point is that salvation is ever God's achievement, never that of humans (verse 27). It is the only answer, the confident answer, to the helpless question, "Then who can be saved?" (verse 26). A paraphrase of this seemingly complex passage (10:23–26) shows that the thought is not difficult to follow: How hard indeed it is for anyone to enter the kingdom, but for rich people it is quite impossible. In fact, humanly speaking, it is impossible for anyone to be saved, rich or not, but with God all things are possible. This is Paul's teaching in Romans.

All attempts to soften the hard sayings of Jesus (verse 25) contradict Mark's obvious intent. The concern throughout verses 17–31 was the problem of wealth in relation to the kingdom of God. The fact that the disciples were reported as being "perplexed" (verse 24) and "astounded" (verse 26) at Jesus' words, together with their question with regard to who can be saved (verse 26), suggests that they believed the prosperity of the rich to be a sign of God's blessing. Mark, however, has presented wealth as a stumbling block, or insurmountable barrier on the way to the kingdom. Can the rich be saved? Jesus acknowledged that salvation for the rich was possible, but it was possible only through the power of God (verse 27). The point of this saying is that God will have to work a miracle of conversion in the hearts of the rich in order for them to be saved. It is so hard for those with wealth to divest themselves of their material possessions, and the security and power that seem to come with them, that it will take divine intervention to free the rich from their bondage.

The passage that follows (10:28–31) directs the reader's attention to a group of individuals, Peter and the other disciples, who have overcome the lure of possessions and left their families, homes, and occupations to follow Jesus in a life of discipleship. This does not mean, however, that to be a disciple one must be destitute. Jesus promised that those who forsake all for the kingdom will receive a hundredfold in this life. Despite his pattern as itinerant prophet and teacher, Jesus was no ascetic. The life of the poor, with its hardship and suffering, is not set forth in Mark's Gospel as an ideal for the Christian disciple; but neither is the desire for possessions or the accumulation of wealth a reflection of the will of God.

The disciples had left everything; Peter stated the fact with some complacency (verse 28). His implicit question is made explicit in Matt 19:27: "What then will we have?" The items listed (verse 29), given disjunctively, included all possessions under the heads of home, relatives, and property. Significant is an omission in verse 30. Verse 29 reads, "no one who has left house or brothers or sisters or mother or father or children or fields," while verse 30 reads, "houses, brothers and sisters, mothers and children, and fields." "Fathers" are absent! This is a factor in the growing evidence that Jesus had envisaged a discipleship of equals. He surely did not have in mind (given his distinctive view of authority) a patriarchal model, with its pattern of domination. "With persecutions" (verse 30)—this may be meant to give an ironical twist to the hundredfold "reward" for total renunciation. More simply, it reflects the harsh reality of Christian experience. Yet, despite the afflictions that assailed them, early Christians found abundant compensation in their new brotherhood and sisterhood (see Romans 16:13). The saying of verse 31 occurs also, in a wholly different context, in Matthew 20:16 and Luke 13:30. We have no way of knowing with certainty the original import of the saying. Mark, seemingly, understands it to mean that while the rich and prosperous are first in this world, those who have left all things (and consequently are last here below) will be first in the world to come.

False Religion

In 12:37b–40, the Markan Jesus issues a warning against the "scribes." The Gospel presentation of scribes paints them, in our terms, as theologians and lawyers. They prided themselves on their expertise and on their meticulous religious observance. On both scores they (or some among them) invited and received deference. To that end they affected distinctive dress (see Matthew 23:1–7). It ought surely to be of more than academic interest that the Jesus tradition is critical of "churchly" dress and "ecclesiastical" lifestyle. The scribes claimed the "best seats" in the synagogues: directly in front of the ark containing the sacred scrolls and facing the people. The charge of verse 40 is more serious. "They devour widows' houses and for the sake of appearance say long prayers." In other words, they are accused of exploiting the social and financial vulnerability of widows. Judaism had some scathing condemnation of such conduct. The sweeping tone of the charges here, however, reflects the animosity between the Christian movement and official Judaism, an animosity more trenchantly expressed in Matthew 23.

This portrait of the scribes stands, and was meant to stand, in sharp contrast to the attitude and conduct of Christian leaders (9:33–37; 10:42–45). Yet what has been, and continues to be, the reality in the church? Elaborate dress, honorific titles, signs of deference, places of honor at religious and civic functions! It is not easy to see a difference between such practice and the conduct of scribes outlined and censured here in verses 38–39.

Traditions

As the text stands, a precise incident lay behind Jesus' dispute with the Pharisees and scribes (Mark 7:1–23): they had observed that the disciples of Jesus did not practice the ritual washing of hands before meals. In their eyes this constituted a transgression of the "tradition of the elders"—the *halakah*, the oral law. These Pharisaic traditions claimed to interpret and complete the Mosaic Law and were regarded as equally authoritative and binding. Later rabbis would claim that the "ancestral law" constituted a second, oral, law given, together with the written law, to Moses on Mount Sinai.

In responding to the charge of neglecting one observance (verse 5), Jesus turned the debate on to a wider issue: the relative worth of Mosaic Law and oral law. He cited Isaiah 29:13 (in its Greek form!) against the Pharisees, drawing a parallel between "human precepts" of which Isaiah spoke and the "human traditions" on which the Pharisees counted. Jesus rejected the oral law because it was the creation of men (not the word of God) and because it could and did conflict with the law of God. The oral law had put casuistry above love. He instanced (verses 9–13) a glaring example of casuistry run wild: a precise vow of dedication. A man might declare *korban*—that is, dedicated to God—the property or capital that, by right, should go to the support of his elderly parents. Property thus made over by vow took on a sacred character; the parents had no more claim on it. In point of fact, such a vow was a legal fiction, a mean way of avoiding filial responsibility. But it was a vow and, as such, in rabbinical eyes, was binding and could not be dispensed. In this manner, a solemn duty enjoined by the Torah was set aside. Jesus could multiply examples, he declared (verse 13) He was aware that one whose mind runs to casuistry loses all sense of proportion. Minute detail becomes more and more important. Law and observance become an obsession. People are defined in terms of conformity or of "sinful" departure from it. It is a disease far worse than miserliness. For the most part, the miser nurses his own misery. Casuists are regularly in positions of authority and make life miserable for others, especially the vulnerable.

The New Law of Purity (7:14–23)

The principle of clean and unclean (a strictly ritual principle) was at the root of Jewish concern with ritual purity. A saying of Jesus (authentic in light of the criterion of discontinuity, it was out of step with the currently accepted view) struck at the very distinction of clean and unclean, of sacred and secular: "There is nothing outside a person that by going in can defile, but the things that come out are what defile" (verse 15). At one stroke Jesus had set aside the whole concept of ritual impurity. Holiness does not lie in the sphere of "clean" over against "unclean"; it is not in the realm of *things* but in the realm of *conduct*. It is to be found in the human heart and is a matter of human responsibility. Mark's parenthetical comment—"Thus he declared all foods clean" (verse 19)—correctly caught the nuance of the saying. It is, more generally, a flat denial that any external things or circumstances can separate one from God (see Romans 8:38–39). We can be separated from God only through our own attitude and behavior. In a Gentile-Christian setting, this saying of verse 15 was provided with a commentary (verses 17–22). The first half—nothing outside a person can defile— is explained in verses 18b–19, and the second part of the verse—it is what comes out of a person that makes one unclean—is developed in verses 20–23.

Lists of sins and vices (verses 21–22) were commonplace in Hellenistic popular philosophy. For other similar lists in the New Testament, see Galatians 5:19–21; Romans 1:29–31; 1 Peter 4:3. In his text the first six nouns in Mark's list are in the plural, indicating evil acts: acts of sexual vice, theft, murder, adultery, acts of coveting or lust, and wickedness in general. The six following vices are: deceit, wantonness, envy (literally, an "evil eye"), slander, pride (arrogance), and folly (the stupidity of one who lacks moral judgment). Verse 23 simply explains the phrase "what comes out of a person" (verse 20). "All these evil things" are found within oneself; it is these and not anything external to one that defile. That defilement can come only from within is emphasized by the repeated phrase "defile a person," which brackets the list of sins and vices. In this discussion as a whole (verses 6–23) it was made clear to Gentile Christians that being followers of Christ did not involve them in observance of Jewish practices. "The Way" (see Acts 9:2; 19:9, 23) is truly open to all men and women.

Jesus' contrast between word of God and human law, and his emphatic assertion of the priority of the former, are obviously of abiding validity and moment. In our day we face a particularly painful instance of a clash of interests. The Eucharist is surely central to Christianity. The Christian people of God have a God-given right to the Eucharist. Increasingly, the Christian people are being deprived of the Eucharist as a consequence of a man-made regulation: mandatory celibacy. Ideology takes precedence over theology and pastoral concern. What, now, of the challenge of Jesus: "You abandon the commandment of God and hold to human tradition" (7:8)?

Ambition versus Service

The third and lengthiest prediction of the passion (10:33–34) corresponds very closely with the stages of the passion narrative in Mark 15. Sadly, the stark words fell on ears deafened by selfish ambition (verses 35–37). The request of the brothers James and John is naively direct: the first places in Jesus' messianic kingdom, no less! When Jesus asked them whether they had considered the price to be paid for a share in his glory, they responded with brash confidence (verse 39). "The cup that I drink"—in the Old Testament "cup" is a symbol both of joy and of suffering. Our context demands the latter sense and, specifically, the idea of redemptive messianic suffering (see Mark 8:31; 9:31; 14:36; John 18:11). "The baptism that I am baptized with": the "baptism" is the passion which will "plunge" Jesus into a sea of suffering. The brothers are being told: you do not know the price that must be paid to share my glory. Here, indeed, it is like master like servant—and Jesus must suffer these things before entering into his glory (Luke 24:26). They must be prepared to accept the full implication of following Jesus. The power of the risen Lord would in due course break through the self-interest of James and John and give backbone to their facile enthusiasm; they will indeed courageously walk in the way of their master. We may well find something of ourselves in this pair.

The other ten were no less uncomprehending than James and John; they were indignant at being circumvented by the shrewd twins (verse 41). This was an appropriate occasion for another lesson in discipleship (verses 42–45). Jesus solemnly asserted that, in the community of his disciples, there is no place for ambition. His church is a human society; there is place for authority, for leaders. But those who lead will serve their brothers and sisters: the spirit of authority is *diakonia* ("service"). Surely Jesus had intended the paradox and had asked for it to be taken seriously. He first outlined the accepted standard of civil authority: domination, with leaders lording it over their subjects, making their presence felt in all areas of life (10:42). Then (verse 43) he asserted that this was not, positively not, to be the pattern for those who professed to follow him. Jesus stood authority on its head. Greatness would be measured by service: the leader will be slave (*doulos*) of the community. There could be no place at all for styles and trappings and exercise of authority after the model of civil powers and princes. Is there anything in the Gospels quite as categorical as this demand?

The ground of the paradoxical behavior required of disciples is to be found in the example of the Son of Man (verse

45). Here this distinctive authority *(exousia)* with its firm stamp of *diakonia* ("service") is given christological underpinning. The saying "For the Son of Man came not to be served but to serve, and to give his life a ransom for many [all]" specifies in what sense Jesus would "serve" people: he would give his life for them. *Lytron* (ransom) was originally a commercial term: the ransom is the price that must be paid to redeem a pledge, to recover a pawned object, or to free a slave. In the Septuagint (the Greek version of the Old Testament), the term is predicated metaphorically of God, who is frequently said to have bought, acquired, ransomed his people (for example, Psalm 49:8; Isaiah 63:4). In its Markan form the saying is related to Isaiah 53:10–11 and "ransom" is to be understood in the sense of the Hebrew word *asham* of Isaiah 53:10, an "offering for sin," an atonement offering. By laying down his life for a humankind enslaved to sin, Jesus fulfilled the word about the Servant in Isaiah 53:10–11. Jesus had paid the universal debt; he gave his life to redeem all others. But this is metaphor, not crude commerce. The death of Jesus, in the Father's purpose and in the Son's acceptance, was a gesture of sheer love: "Surely, they will respect my Son...not what I want, but what you want" (Mark 12:6; 14:36). Any suggestion that the death of the Son was the literal payment of a debt, the placating of an offended deity, is a tragic misperception. God is ever motivated by love, not "justice."

This word of Jesus was clear. Would it be heard? Not throughout Christian history. But it was heard in the Jerusalem of Jesus' day, and heard by the Roman power, heard as subversive of authority. Jesus was dangerous and had to be silenced. His teaching was political dynamite.

SUMMARY

Christians may be children of God, but they are truly such only on condition that they understand what it means and live with its demands. Mark's own understanding of discipleship was the same as that of Paul: "If children, then heirs, heirs of God and joint heirs with Christ—if, in fact, we suffer with him so that we may also be glorified with him" (Romans 8:17). His preoccupation with discipleship follows hard on his concern with Christology. The way of discipleship had been firmly traced by Jesus himself. "If any want to be my followers, let them deny themselves and take up their cross and follow me" (8:34). For Mark there is no other way of discipleship. Following the path of the victory of Christ, the Christian is not preserved from suffering and even death, but is sustained through suffering and death.

Mark assuredly looked beyond the ministry of Jesus, to the community of his concern. He reminded those followers of a rejected and crucified Messiah that it should not surprise that they, too, were called upon to suffer (13:9–13). The cross had turned the values of the world upside down—it is indeed a "stumbling-block" and "foolishness" (see 1 Corinthians 1:23). They must be steadfast in face of persecution. They must not be ashamed of Jesus' way of humiliation and suffering and death if they do not want the glorious Son of Man to be ashamed of them at his coming. And they hear his comforting assurance, "Surely, I am coming soon" (Revelation 22:20; see Mark 9:1).

The second prediction of the passion (Mark 9:30–32) is followed by further instruction on discipleship. It was needed because in verses 33 through 34 the disciples' lack of understanding is blatant. Although disciples of a master so soon to suffer bitter humiliation and death, they are all too humanly involved in petty squabbling over precedent. The Teacher took his seat and called the Twelve to him. His message was unequivocal: "Whoever wants to be first must be last of all and servant of all" (verse 35). He backed up his word with a prophetic gesture: the presentation of a little child. The manner of it tells much of the delicate sensitivity of Jesus—"taking it in his arms"—a touch proper to Mark (see 10:16). "Whoever welcomes one such child in my name welcomes me" (verse 37). "Welcome" means loving service of the weaker members of the community, those who stand in greatest need of being served. A Christian is one baptized "into the name of" Jesus (Matthew 28:19; 1 Corinthians 1:13, 15), so becoming his. That is why one meets (serves) Christ himself in the disciple and meets the Father in Christ. It is the dignity of Christian service. Mark has made the point that the revelation of Jesus cannot be acknowledged by one who is not ready to enter into the spirit of discipleship and thereby become "last" and "servant." One would hope that the Christian of today is attuned to the unambiguous message of this word of Jesus: greatness in his church is found in *diakonia* ("service") and only there. A first step is to have discerned this. It is the right of the people of God to have such service. It is their right to demand that leadership in the Church, at every level, be service, not in word but in deed.

THE TRIUMPH OF FAILURE

The fact remains that "for Jesus his violent death was historically a fiasco."[2] What is implied is a distinction between the terms *historical* and *historic*. One can label as "historical" anything that happens in history. An "historic" event is a happening of far-reaching historical significance. The truth of the matter is that his death marked Jesus as *historically* a failure. Jesus was executed on the order of a Roman provincial official: an alleged troublemaker in that bothersome province of Judea had been dealt with. The incident did not raise a ripple in imperial affairs. Yet history has shown that this execution was an event of *historic* proportions: two thousand years later, its ripples flow stronger than ever.

Let us be clear about it. The Romans and the Jewish Sanhedrin had effectively closed the "Jesus case." The aims and message of Jesus, and his life itself, had ended in death. His prophetic voice had been muzzled. That is failure. The question is "*Why* had Jesus been silenced?" It was because he had unflinchingly lived and preached God's love for humankind. That is why he had table fellowship with sinners, why he sought to free men and women from the tyranny of religion, why he, at every turn, bore witness to the true God. He might, in face of the threatening opposition, have packed up and gone home to Nazareth. That would have been *real* failure. But he would not be turned from witnessing to God's love. They might take his life, but to his last breath he would witness. "Father, forgive them"—there is the victory. What Jesus tells us is that failure is *not* the last word—that is, as God views failure.

From God's point of view, in the fate of Jesus there can be no talk of failure. This is what John brings out, dramatically, in his Gospel. He undoubtedly knew the synoptic tradition but he chose to turn its tragedy into comedy. What is important for us in his presentation is that he has stressed what the other evangelists imply: failure is not the last word. But what Mark has done is at least of equal importance: he has shown that a sense of failure, even for Jesus, is a grievous human experience.

There is a further point. Too often the resurrection of Jesus is presented as a rescue operation. As someone has put it graphically, it is like the climax of a Western movie when the beleaguered wagon train is saved by a troop of U.S. cavalry riding out of the sunset. The truth is that resurrection is inherent in the life and death of Jesus. His "failure" was his total commitment to God and to humankind. That historical moment of failure on the cross was God's overcoming of human failure. If Paul can declare of the Christian that nothing in all creation can separate him or her from the love of God (Romans 8:39), then a death motivated only by love cannot, for a moment, cut off Jesus from his God. The human cry of God-forsakenness is heavy with *feeling*. The reality is quite other: never were Son and Father more wholly one. The ultimate helplessness of death was disclosed. "God raised him up, having loosed the pangs of death, *because it was not possible for him to be held by it*" (Acts 2:24).

NOTES

CHAPTER 3

1. For this discussion I am indebted to Francis J. Moloney, *The Gospel of Mark* (Peabody, MA: Hendrickson, 2002), 350–352.

CHAPTER 4

1. See Wilfrid J. Harrington, O.P., *Jesus Our Brother* (New York: Paulist Press, 2010), 13–15.

2. John P. Meier, *A Marginal Jew.* Vol. 2. Mentor, Message, and Miracles (New York: Doubleday, 1994), 512.

3. The criterion of multiple attestation focuses on sayings or deeds of Jesus present in more than one literary source (for example, Mark, Paul, and John). The criterion of coherence maintains that sayings or deeds of Jesus which merge well with data established by other criteria are presumably historical.

4. Meier, *A Marginal Jew*, 406–407. I am indebted to Meier's book for much of this discussion of Jesus as an exorcist.

CHAPTER 5

1. Francis J. Moloney, *The Gospel of Mark* (Peabody, MA: Hendrickson, 2002), 354.

CHAPTER 6

1. Meier, *A Marginal Jew*. Vol. 3. Companions and Competitors (New York: Doubleday, 2001), 72; see 40–124.

2. Edward Schillebeckx, *Christ: The Experience of Jesus as Lord* (New York: Crossroad, 1981), 829.

GLOSSARY

I hope that reference to this glossary will spare the reader the chore of searching out in the text the meaning of some recurring terms.

Allegory - Allegory (in which the details of a story have symbolic value, such as in the Wicked Tenants [Mark 12:1–8]) is extended metaphor and, as such, is a story that has both a literal and a metaphorical level. An allegorical story can well be a parable, as in the example cited. There are several allegorical parables in the Gospels.

Apocalyptic - "Apocalypse," from the Greek *apocalypsis* ("revelation"), designates a type of Jewish literature that flourished from about 200 BC to 100 AD. As a literary form it is presented as a revelation, or series of revelations, of heavenly secrets made to a seer and conveyed in highly symbolic imagery. It is a crisis literature. The biblical apocalypses are the book of Daniel (more precisely, Daniel 7—12) and the Revelation of John. Apocalypticism is the worldview of an

161

apocalyptic movement. In this view it is taken for granted that a supernatural world stands above our earthly world. That heavenly world is the "real" world. There is a twofold dualism: vertical, the world above and our world, and horizontal, our age and the age to come. There is always a definitive eschatological judgment: the final clash between good and evil, issuing in the total victory of God and the end of evil. Apocalyptic ideas pervade the New Testament.

Apostle - The Christian mission was carried out by "apostles"—those "sent out" (*apostellein*) from the Christian communities. Acts 13:1–4, the designation and sending out by the Antioch community of Barnabas and Saul, is an eloquent instance of this. There has been an unfortunate confusion of "Twelve" and "apostle." The Twelve were "apostles" in the sense that they had been "sent out" by Jesus. "Apostle" has a much wider range than the Twelve, however.

Christology - Christology is the theological understanding of Jesus. In Jesus of Nazareth, God is really and truly present. That is the great Christian truth. But to seek to define the mysterious nature of Jesus is a precarious endeavor. For centuries it has been assumed that the fifth-century council of Chalcedon had spoken the definitive christological word when it answered, in the affirmative, the question of whether God's salvation had been given, once for all, in the man Jesus. Because the answer had to be Yes, and because salvation is of God, it had to be asserted, in the theological language of the day, that God himself was present in the man Jesus. That had been said, long before, by Paul: "God was in Christ, reconciling the world to himself" (2 Corinthians 11:25). In this sense, too, the Christology of Mark can be understood.

Covenant - Originally a treaty graciously "granted" by an overlord. God gave a covenant to his people at Sinai ("I am your God; you are my people") sealed and ratified in the blood of a sacrificial victim. Jeremiah spoke of a "new covenant" (Jeremiah 31:31–34). This new covenant with the new people of God was given through Jesus and sealed in his blood (see 1 Corinthians 11:25).

Disciple - Jesus gathered around himself a group of committed disciples, some of whom were also active in the early church. Distinctive features of this initial discipleship were as follows: Jesus took the initiative in calling; "following" meant literal, physical following of an itinerant preacher; disciples were warned that they might face suffering and hostility. The evidence is clear that some women did follow Jesus during his ministry in Galilee and accompanied him on his last journey to Jerusalem (see Mark 15:40–41). "Disciple" is an inclusive term.

Divine Passive - Reverence for God is a marked feature of Jewish religion. The unique name of the God of Israel, Yahweh, was not pronounced; "the Lord" was substituted. Furthermore, there was reticence in the use of the generic term *God*. Typical is Matthew's "kingdom of heaven" for "kingdom of God." Another technique was use of the passive form of the verb. So, for instance, "For to those who have, more will be given" (Mark 4:25) means, "God will give more."

Eschatological - Pertaining to the *eschaton*, the End. Eschatology refers to the new age, the transformation of our world. But with the coming of Jesus, this new age has already begun; we await the consummation. In the preaching of Jesus, the kingdom of God is eschatological: the definitive intervention of God, his kingly reign, is (in Jesus) a present reality. It seems that Jesus thought of himself as the eschatological prophet.

Kerygma - The "heralding" or "preaching" of the good news: the missionary preaching of the good news to Jews and Gentiles.

Kingdom of God - The precise phrase *kingdom of God* occurs only once in the Old Testament, in Wisdom 10:10. The expression was not current in Judaism at the time of Jesus and was not widely used by early Christians. "Kingdom of God" is found predominantly in the Synoptic Gospels (Matthew, Mark, and Luke) and then almost always on the lips of Jesus. It was evidently central to Jesus' proclamation. Israel regarded God as universal king. And there was the expectation that God's reign would soon be manifested over the whole world. Jesus spoke, in the main, of a future kingdom: God will reveal himself in power and glory. There is evidence that Jesus also spoke of the kingdom as in some way already present in his own words and deeds. When we consider that the kingdom of God is not primarily a state or place, but rather the dynamic event of God coming in power to rule his people Israel in the end time, it is not surprising that the precise relationship between the future and present kingdom is not specified. That is why Jesus can speak of the kingdom as both imminent and yet present. In Jesus' eyes, his healings and exorcisms were part of the eschatological drama that was already underway and that God was about to bring to its conclusion. The important point is that Jesus deliberately chose to proclaim that the display of miraculous power throughout his ministry was a preliminary and partial realization of God's kingly rule.

Messiah - From a Hebrew Word meaning "anointed." In Greek it is rendered *Christos,* whence "Christ." In Jewish expectation the Messiah would be God's instrument (not a divine figure) in ushering in his kingdom. The expectation is a development of the promise to David in 2 Samuel 7:11–16—the expectation of a royal Messiah. In the New Testament, Jesus is "son of David." It is unlikely that Jesus himself ever claimed to be the Messiah. It is also very likely that Jesus' opponents may have understood him and his followers to claim that he was the Messiah. After the resurrection, of course, Jesus was, by his followers, regularly called the Messiah—Jesus Christ (Messiah). But he was a paradoxical Messiah: one who suffered and died on a cross, not the triumphalist royal messiah of popular expectation.

Messianic Secret - It was firmly Mark's view that no human being could acknowledge in faith and truth that Jesus is the Son of God before the paradoxical revelation of his identity through his death on the cross. Throughout Mark's Gospel we find Jesus repeatedly imposing silence in reference to his identity or role. This is Mark's "Messianic Secret." It really is a misnomer. The element of secrecy concerns not Jesus' messiahship but his identity as Son of God. This was recognized and professed by the centurion at the cross (15:39).

Parable - A parable is a brief story with two levels of meaning. For instance, at first sight, the Sower looks like an agricultural vignette. Its true meaning has to do with reception of the Gospel message. The second level of meaning is always the essential one. The purpose of a parable is to challenge decision and invite action.

Parousia - The Greek word *parousia* means "presence" or "arrival." In the ancient Greek-speaking world it was used of the ceremonial visit of a ruler or of the apparition of a god. In the New Testament, it is used of the "appearance" or coming of the glorified Christ at the close of salvation history. It expresses, in dramatic fashion, faith in a final act of God marking the goal of human history, and the establishment, in its fullness, of the kingdom of God. After New Testament times this came to be known, somewhat unhelpfully, as the Second Coming of Christ. The earliest Christians expected this consummation in their own time. And the expectation may be, and is, often present without use of the term *parousia*.

Pharisees - The Pharisees formed a religious and political grouping of devout Jews that emphasized detailed study and observance of the Law of Moses. They also possessed a normative body of tradition—the traditions of the "fathers" or "elders." While they acknowledged that some of these legal rules and practices went beyond the Law, they maintained that such practices were, nevertheless, God's will for Israel. They actively engaged in trying to convince ordinary Jews to observe these practices in their daily life. Much of what is attributed to Pharisaic teaching refers to legal rulings or opinions regarding concrete behavior (*halakoth*) in matters of purity rules, Sabbath observance, tithing, marriage, and divorce. The Pharisees lacked political power but would have had some political influence. As a major religious force, they enjoyed the respect of the people. After 70 AD and the destruction of the Jerusalem Temple by the Romans, as practically the only religious group to have survived the Jewish War, their influence would have increased. All four Gospels attest to frequent contact of Jesus with Pharisees throughout his ministry. Not surprisingly, this relationship was one of tension because he and they addressed the same constituency. Jesus would have challenged them directly and in parable. Yet the Gospels acknowledge that some Pharisees were willing to give Jesus a serious hearing (see, for example, Luke 7:36–50; John 3:1–2). It is noteworthy that Pharisees are practically absent in all Gospel passion narratives. The death of Jesus was brought about historically not by Pharisees, but by a religious and political alliance of Jerusalem priesthood and Roman political authority.

Pronouncement Story - This is a brief story leading to a notable saying of Jesus; the story is designed to focus on the "punch line." For example, in Mark 12:13–17 the saying "Render to Caesar what is Caesar's and to God what is God's" is effectively emphasized.

Scribes - The word *scribe* in Hebrew, Greek and other languages had a wide range of meaning. Scribes wrote, copied, and guarded records for tax and military purposes, annals for government archives, and religious texts. Palestinian scribes in Jesus' time were, in fact, bureaucrats. In Jerusalem they assisted the priests in judicial and religious proceedings in the

Sanhedrin. They would have played a secretarial role and, as in a modern civil service, some might have had a measure of influence. On the whole, they were "retainers." The Gospels seem to suggest that the scribes, as a homogenous group, formed part of a united front against Jesus. This is not historically accurate.

Sadducees - The Sadducees were a small group of priestly and lay aristocrats based in Jerusalem. They were theologically conservative, adhering to the clear teaching of the Torah, or Pentateuch (see Acts 26:6–10). The Sadducees appear rarely in the Synoptic Gospels—only once in Mark (12:18–27)—and are completely absent from the writings of John and Paul.

Son of God - The New Testament church confessed Jesus as Son of God, and in doing so attributed to Jesus a unique relationship to God. Was the title *Son of God* bestowed on Jesus during his lifetime? It was used, in association with *Messiah*, by the high priest (Mark 14:61), but the exchange between the high priest and Jesus (14:61–62) reflects the Christology of the evangelist. Jesus did not refer to himself directly as Son of God.

Son of Man - "The Son of Man" occurs more than eighty times in the Gospels and, practically without exception, as a self-designation by Jesus. Jesus used the phrase in a neutral sense to refer to himself indirectly. He likely had in mind as well the "one like a son of man" of Daniel 7:13. Jesus was the human one, serving God's purpose, and looking to vindication at the completion of his mission. Early Christians embraced the phrase, now regarded as a title. There are three types of Son of Man sayings in the Gospels: those which refer to the earthly activity of the Son of Man (Mark 2:10, 28), those which refer to the suffering Son of Man (see, for example, Mark 8:31), and those which refer to the future glory and *parousia* of the Son of Man (see, for example, Mark 14:62).

Torah - Commonly translated as "Law," but better rendered "instruction" or "guide of life," the Torah is basically the Pentateuch, the first five books of the Old Testament. For the Jews, the Torah was the full expression of God's purpose for his people. Indeed, Law and Lawgiver were practically identical. In this situation, the Torah took on an absolute value, and one could concern oneself exclusively with the law. This was an attitude combated by Jesus, notably in Mark 7.

Twelve, The - From his disciples Jesus chose a core group: the Twelve (see, for example, Mark 6:7). The mission of the Twelve (Mark 6:6–13) was a prophetic gesture; it symbolized the process of regathering. After the election of Matthias to bring the number back to twelve following the departure of Judas (Acts 1:15–26), it was evidently understood that the number twelve as it pertained to this core group of disciples was symbolic and pertained to the eschatological mission of Jesus (see *Apostle*).

SELECT BIBLIOGRAPHY

GENERAL

Brown, R. E. *The Death of the Messiah*. Two volumes. New York, NY: Doubleday, 1994.

Dunn, J.D.G. *Jesus Remembered: Christianity in the Making*. Vol. 1. Grand Rapids, MI: Eerdmans, 2003.

Meier, J. P. *A Marginal Jew*, Vol. 1: *Rethinking the Historical Jesus*. Vol. 2: *Mentor, Message, and Miracles* New York, NY: Doubleday, 1991, 1994.

MARK

Achtemeier, P. J. *Mark*. Philadelphia, PA: Fortress Press, 1975.

Donahue, J. R. and Harrington, D. J. *The Gospel of Mark*. Collegeville, MN: Liturgical Press, 2002.

Harrington, W. *What Was Mark At? The Gospel of Mark: A Commentary*. Dublin, Ire.: The Columba Press, 2008.

MAR 13 20

Hooker, M. D. *The Gospel According to St. Mark.* Peabody, MA: Hendrickson, 1991.

Kingsbury, J. D. *Conflict in Mark: Jesus, Authorities, Disciples.* Minneapolis, MN: Fortress, 1989.

Moloney. F. J. *The Gospel of Mark: A Commentary.* Peabody, MA: Hendrickson, 2002.

Rhoads, D., and Michie, D. *Mark as Story.* Philadelphia, PA: Fortress Press, 1982.

Schnelle, U. *Theology of the New Testament.* Grand Rapids, MI: Baker Academic, 2007, "Mark," 399–429.

Senior, D. *The Passion of Jesus in the Gospel of Mark.* Wilmington, DE: M. Glazier, 1985.

Thurston, B. B. *Preaching Mark.* Minneapolis, MN: Fortress Press, 2002.